THE
RAILWAY
POLICEMAN'S
CASEBOOK

RICHARD STACPOOLE-RYDING

AMBERLEY

First published 2016

Amberley Publishing
The Hill, Stroud,
Gloucestershire, GL5 4EP

www.amberley-books.com

ISBN: 978 1 4456 5646 5 (print)
ISBN: 978 1 4456 5647 2 (ebook)

British Library Cataloguing in Publication Data.
A catalogue record for this book is available from the British Library.

Typeset in 10pt on 13pt Celeste.
Typesetting by Amberley Publishing.
Printed in the UK.

Contents

Foreword

It is my pleasure to write a few words to this excellent book, which takes a look at crime on our national railways over the decades.

It never ceases to amaze me, the wide ambit of offences that have been committed on Britain's railway and dock systems. As this publication illustrates, everything from murder and manslaughter to robbery and theft, forgery and fraud, vandalism and terrorism features in crime statistics of the earlier railway police forces.

The same can be said about railway crime in more recent times. But policing in any era brings with it challenges of a transient population, making it that much more difficult in the detection and apprehension of criminals.

It is worth also reflecting on the work of those earlier railway detectives and the obstacles that they faced in bringing offenders to justice, for they did not have the advances in communications, science and technology that today's police enjoy. They certainly had their work cut out in detecting and prosecuting offenders.

As a retired British Transport Police officer, I recall being on a detective training course in the 1970s along with colleagues from Home Department police forces when I was tasked with giving a talk on railway crime. Having done a bit of research I came up with a whole range of cases of interest, spanning many years, and it became very apparent that practicably every conceivable crime in the criminal textbook had been committed at some time or other within the jurisdiction of the railway police. The perpetrators of crime certainly did not (and still do not) respect the boundaries between our towns, cities and local communities and the nation's railways. Perhaps one crime that I'm not aware of being committed on the railway is that of infanticide, but I stand to be corrected on that.

I'd like to point out that crime on today's railways is relatively low and we can proudly boast that Britain's railway system is by far one of the safest in the world. With modern technology that wasn't available to our predecessors in the earlier railway police forces, the emphasis on crime prevention today is very much at the forefront of BTP's approach to policing in the twenty-first century.

I sincerely hope the reader of this book doesn't get the feeling of a crime-ridden environment when visiting stations or by travelling by train or tube. For that is certainly not the case. I would ask the reader to instead reflect on the historical aspects of *The Railway Policeman's Casebook* and enjoy the fascinating and interesting crimes committed in a bygone era and portrayed here.

John Owen
Chairman
British Transport Police History Group

Preface

Researching and writing this book has been an interesting journey. Reading cases covering every conceivable crime committed on the railways from the early days to the 1980s and choosing cases representing the work of the railway policeman has been a difficult one. There have been many cases worthy of recording but space has precluded this and it is hoped that those that have made up the contents of this book will be representative of the work encountered by officers of the various railway police forces throughout the decades. I have kept the name policeman and policewoman where this was the accepted title for officers and also the name of offences at the time of the case in to keep the atmosphere of the case.

Every attempt has been made to seek permission for copyrighted material used in the book. However, if I have inadvertently used copyrighted material without permission or acknowledgement I apologise and will make the necessary correction at the first opportunity.

Acknowledgements

I would like to acknowledge the support of Sue Batters and Ed Thompson. Sue has spent numerous hours judiciously reading the drafts and making corrections and suggestions. Without Sue's input and interest, writing this book would have been much harder. Ed has spent many hours travelling the length and breadth of the country to the locations where some of crimes were committed and taking photographs for inclusion in the book. To both I owe an eternal debt of gratitude. I would like to thank John Owen for his foreword, Malcom Clegg and Viv Head for their assistance in the chapter 'The Murder of Police Officers on the Railway' and Inspector Michael 'Dan' Tanner from the British Transport Police, whose bravery is recorded in 'The Railway Policeman Faces Danger'. A thank you to my editor from Amberley Publishing, Connor Stait, who first approached me about writing this book, and has supported me throughout the process. I must also thank The British Transport Police History Group whose archive of the British Transport Commission Police and British Transport Police Journals has been the inspiration for the book. Any errors or omissions are mine and mine alone. Finally my partner Nicola and son Christopher, who have supported me and endured long hours of solitude while I have been writing.

1

The Murder of Police Officers on the Railway

The crime of murder is abhorrent and distressing, not only to the victim's family and friends but to the public. Fortunately, the murder of police officers in the execution of their duty is not an everyday occurrence in this country but, when it does happen, it is met with shock and disbelief by colleagues throughout the country and by the general public. There have been few murders of officers who police the railways of this country, but the following three cases record the bravery and dedication to duty, with disregard to their own safety, that officers show in the course of their work.

The Murder of Police Constable Joseph Byrne

Notorious gangs have always had their own identity, often linked to the *modus operandi* they employ to carry out their particular branch of crime. One such gang, operating in 1885, were known as 'The Ladder Gang' and comprised four men, Anthony Benjamin Rudge, John Martin, James Baker and William Baker, who was no relation. They all had a long criminal background and were considered to be dangerous and unpredictable. Rudge was a dog trainer and dog thief who had been in prison many times and was, at the time of this incident, wanted for robbery in Brixton, South London. John Martin was another career criminal who had been imprisoned on numerous occasions and was wanted for the murder of a police inspector in Essex. James Baker was a well-known and convicted receiver of stolen goods. William Baker was known for theft with violence and had a string of convictions and terms of imprisonment.

On 27 October 1885, the gang travelled to Gretna Green on a special train hired by the Longtown Coursing Meeting. On arrival at the station, they deposited their bags in the station master's office and carried out a recce of the local area, making enquiries about Netherby Hall, which was located a few miles away from Carlisle.

This was the home of Sir Frederick Graham and his family, who were in residence at the time. It was the gang's intention to burgle the hall, and they booked in at The Bush Hotel in Longtown where, over dinner and using the information they had gathered, they made plans for the following night, when the deed was to be done. The next afternoon, James Baker collected one of their bags from Gretna Green station and met his colleagues in a public house called The Graham Arms, situated close by. While there, they made a wax impression of a key, but were seen by a local man who was curious about the new arrivals in Gretna. The man informed the publican but the matter was soon dismissed. The key later turned out to be that of Lady Graham's room; it was never established how this came to be in the gang's possession. Later in the day, James Baker returned to the station and made arrangements to forward the same case he had picked up earlier to Carlisle for the attention of a Mr A. Smith.

When evening had drawn in, the gang made their way to Netherby Hall, entered the grounds and, by using a ladder, climbed through the window into Lady Hermione Graham's room and locked the door with the key they had made earlier. They went about the business of searching the room and then left, taking with them a large amount of valuable jewellery. At about 8 p.m. one of the maids had occasion to go to her mistress's room, found the door locked and informed the butler who, after looking around, found the ladder the gang had used *in situ* and entered the room to discover the burglary. Sir Frederick was told, and he sent word to the police in Longtown and began his own search of the area for the gang. The police in Carlisle were alerted and asked to keep all roads under observation.

The gang made a good escape initially, but the plan was to start unravelling when they were spotted near Longtown by a sergeant and constable of the local constabulary. The officers stopped the gang, who fired two shots from a revolver, after which they began running away. The officers followed swiftly and were fired upon again, both being wounded, one in the shoulder and the other in the thigh, as the gang scrambled down a railway embankment and began walking along the line towards Carlisle. They made their way to Gosling Dyke and, at about 11 p.m., were stopped by PC Handley of the local constabulary who, when faced with the revolver, let the gang pass and quickly summoned assistance. The gang were next seen at 2 a.m. the following morning, when the signalman at Dalston Road Crossing on the North Eastern Railway saw three men walking along the track; however, when he opened the signal box door they were alerted and began to run away. PC Fortune, of the local constabulary, had just arrived at the box to inform the signalman of what was happening, so he gave chase but, alas, the three men turned and beat him unconscious. The men scattered and were well away into the night by the time the constable came round and was able to raise the alarm. The search continued into the next day and evidence of where the gang members had been hiding since they were last seen came to light. Two of the gang were reported to have been in a railway goods yard near Carlisle and a bloodstained jemmy was discovered in an empty wagon in the Blencowe goods yard.

The search for the gang continued, and at about 7 p.m. a station master at Southwaite station was approached by a member of the gang, who asked him about trains to London. However, when he appeared unhappy that the next train would be too late for him, the station master became suspicious and sent for the railway police. A few miles to the south at Plumpton, at about 8.25 p.m., the station master there saw three men acting in a suspicious way and, being mindful of the events that had been unfolding, sent a porter to get the railway police. The local constable, PC Joseph Byrne, had also been alerted and went off to find the three men after sending word, via his informant, to get some back up. By this time, two of the gang, Benjamin Rudge and James Baker, had entered The Pack Horse Inn and ordered bread, cheese and beer. They then calmly sat down and ate their food before eventually leaving. It was soon after they left the inn that a shot was heard by a signalman and other people nearby, but it was another half an hour before a man walking past heard a moaning from behind a wall and found PC Byrne lying badly injured. He had been shot through the head. There was little doubt that he had encountered Rudge and Baker, who had shown no compunction in shooting him and leaving him to die, as was the case after he had been found.

The news of Byrne's murder gave fresh energy and determination to the search for the gang. The murder of a policeman then, as today, sent shock waves throughout the police force and general public, and everyone was determined that the murderers would be caught and brought to justice. At about 10 p.m. a constable on duty at a bridge near Penrith spotted three men behaving in a suspicious manner and followed them but lost them in the darkness of the night. A goods train was due to leave Keswick Junction near Penrith and the wagons were searched by the police prior to departure, but there was no sign of the gang. However, the guard, Christopher Gaddes, who was on the train, had been asked to keep a look-out for the gang and, as the train moved off, he saw three men rush from bushes alongside the track and clamber into an empty wagon. Not wanting to tackle the men himself, he threw out messages written on the back of way-bills onto the platforms at Shap and Tebay stations as the train went through. At Shap, one of the messages was found by an engine driver who telegraphed Tebay to stop the train. However, for unknown reasons, the police were not at Tebay and the train continued on its journey. At the next signal, Gaddes stopped the train and, this time, he and a large number of other railway workers, armed with an array of weapons, began searching the wagons. Suddenly, as a result of this action, the gang broke cover and a vicious struggle took place.

John Martin escaped from the melee but was caught by the engine driver who was brutally assaulted for his pains, allowing Martin to run again. However, he was eventually subdued by others and tied to a telegraph pole – a revolver was found on him during a search. Rudge was also captured and tied to a telegraph pole, where he too was found in possession of a revolver that had been recently fired. William Baker was caught and subdued, but James Baker escaped the struggle and fled into the darkness where he hid in another wagon. Two railway workers spotted him getting out of the wagon near Oxenholme and a message was sent of this sighting. At Lancaster station, a guard saw a man acting suspiciously in the goods yard and went to investigate. The man, who turned out to be James Baker, asked him where the train was going but, possibly due to nerves, Baker fluffed his enquiry. The guard challenged him and a fierce struggle took place, after which Baker was eventually restrained, but not before having taken a lot of punishment from the guard and his fellow workers!

Rudge, Martin and William Baker were sent by train to Carlisle where an angry mob had gathered to meet them. The criminals must have been thankful that they were protected, by both the police escort and the large numbers of officers waiting at the station, or they may never have survived the baying crowd's obvious intention to do them harm.

Once the men were safely in custody, the investigating officers found the case that the gang had sent onto Carlisle and, when opened, it was found to contain house-breaking implements and skeleton keys. The jewels were eventually recovered, following a painstaking search of the route the gang had taken; they had thrown them away during their escape while trying to elude the police search teams. Rudge, Martin and James Baker stood trial at the Carlisle Assizes where the

The Carlisle Citadel Assizes court room where the trial of the three Netherby Hall burglars took place.

Right: The condemned cell where Anthony Rudge, John Martin and James Baker were taken from to the place of execution on the gaol roof.

Below: The memorial erected in the place where Police Constable Joseph Byrne was murdered.

The new headstone erected over Police Constable Byrne's grave on the 121st anniversary of his death in 2006.

proceedings took three days, commencing on 18 January 1886. They were found guilty of the murder of PC Joseph Byrne and the burglary at Netherby Hall. All three were sentenced to death and were hanged on 8 February that same year. Before he was hanged, James Martin admitted it was he that had murdered PC Byrne, but in the eyes of the law all three were just as guilty as the man who had fired the shot. William Baker was tried and found not to be so involved in the murder of PC Byrne and was therefore given the lesser sentence of a long period of penal servitude.

PC Joseph Byrne was a popular local bobby and his murder was keenly felt by those who lived on and around his patch. He was given a hero's funeral and a memorial was erected at the place where he was murdered. The inscription reads: 'Here Constable Joseph Byrnes fell on the night of October 29, 1885, shot by the three Netherby burglars whom he single-handed endeavoured to arrest.' Above the inscription is a cross with the words 'Do or Die'. No one can expect a police officer to do more than that.

The Murder of Detective Sergeant Kidd

Railway sidings and goods yards are, at the best of times, dangerous places. For police officers they are not only dangerous, but are difficult areas in which to maintain observations in order to catch thieves; sometimes the combination of these two factors, plus the possibility of violence during the course of a crime, can add up to more tragic circumstances – murder. One such case involved Detective Sergeant Robert Kidd in 1895.

Robert Kidd was considered to be a career officer. He had originally served as a constable in the Manchester City Police Force before he joined the London & North Western Railway Police as a constable in 1885. He worked hard and, two years later in 1887, he was advanced to detective constable and posted to Warrington for a year before he found himself at Liverpool (Edgehill station). He was promoted to detective sergeant and posted to Manchester (Liverpool Road Goods) in 1889. He was now thirty-seven years old, married with seven children, all under the age the age of twelve, and well thought of by senior and junior officers alike.

In July 1895, a series of thefts from goods wagons had been occurring in Wigan goods yard and, after two months, the officer in charge of the case, Detective Constable William Henry Osbourne, was having no success in catching the thieves. DS Kidd was sent to Wigan to assist Osbourne in bringing the case to a conclusion. On 29 September, at 8 p.m., the two officers met at Wigan railway station; the night was clear with a bright moon, making visibility good, and so the officers walked down the line towards the sidings. As they reached Kay's Sidings, Osbourne looked round the corner of a wall and saw a man, later identified as William Halliwell, on his hands and knees. He was obviously acting in a suspicious manner, so the officers went up to Halliwell and, as they spoke to him, he ran off. Osbourne immediately gave chase and caught Halliwell, pinning him against a goods wagon where a struggle ensued, with Osbourne gaining the upper hand and bringing his man down to the ground. At that moment, another man, later identified as William Kearsley, came round from the wagon and fell over Osbourne and Halliwell. Osbourne quickly realised that he was now in serious trouble and drew his truncheon just as a third man appeared carrying a knife, and Osbourne struck a heavy blow to this man's hand. Kearsley and the man ran off into the goods yard while Osbourne continued to struggle with Halliwell for some ten minutes, the result of which was that Halliwell made his escape, taking Osbourne's truncheon with him.

Osbourne recovered himself, then went off in search of Kidd and found him lying on the ground, between the goods wagon and the wall that ran alongside, with blood running down his face. He tried to lift Kidd up but saw he was in a bad way; Kidd was able to gasp, 'Osbourne, is that you? Get me a drink of water.' Osbourne managed to lift him up and carry him a few yards but he was exhausted from his previous struggle and fell to the ground unconscious, with Kidd by his side. Osbourne did not fully recover consciousness until sometime later in hospital. Although he could not recall, Osbourne apparently had made his way to a nearby signal box, where staff raised the alarm by calling the police and then helped the two officers. Kidd was taken to the railway station where he subsequently died.

The crime had been committed on the borders of two police forces, the Wigan Borough Police and the Lancashire County Constabulary, so both forces were advised and attended. Wigan Borough Police was under the direction of Superintendent Macintosh and the county constabulary was under Superintendent Brassington, who had forty officers at his disposal. The LNWR Police were informed and Chief Detective Inspector Richards, DS Davern and DC Buckingham, reporting to Superintendent Elijah Copping, the officer in charge of the LNWR Police, all joined the two forces later. As all three forces had an interest in the crime they decided to work together for the duration of the investigation.

Superintendent Macintosh, who knew the area well, organised the borough and county forces into groups and began a search of the goods yard; the hunt to catch the thieves was on. The goods wagons were searched and it was discovered that the tarpaulin of wagon No. 12315 had been tampered with, and a box containing bottles of sweets had been opened and a bottle dropped nearby. Two other wagons had been interfered with but nothing appeared to have been taken. In the meantime a local doctor, Dr Graham, had been summoned to attend Kidd and had pronounced him dead. On examination, Kidd had nine knife wounds to his face and neck and numerous abrasions and contusions on his head, face, hands, elbows, left arm and right leg. The knife wounds on his neck had severed arteries,

London & North Western
Railway police helmet plate.

Detective Sergeant Robert Kidd.

a puncture wound had cut through his nose and part of his left index finger had been cut off. These horrendous injuries shocked the police and public alike and soon information began to pour in, enabling the police to make three arrests. The first of these was William Kearsley, at 1.30 p.m. the day after the murder, and he was subsequently picked out by Osbourne at an identity parade set up in the hospital where he was recovering. The second man to be arrested was Elijah Winstanley, a collier, on 1 October at 11.55 p.m. and, finally, William Halliwell was arrested shortly afterwards and, fearing for his life, he decided to turn Queen's evidence. All three were charged with the wilful murder of Robert Kidd and inflicting grievous bodily harm on William Osbourne.

The accused men duly appeared at Wigan Borough Police Court, where a Mr Kershaw was prosecuting for the LNWR Company. During the opening speech, Mr Kershaw was interrupted by Winstanley who shouted out, 'Kill me. Kill me. Go on, it's murder. I did it. I did it. It's me. I didn't intend killing him.' It was quite apparent to the court that Winstanley was in a hysterical state when he made this outburst.

During the hearing, it was clear that the men had every intention of stealing from the railway wagons. All three men had met in a public house called the New Inn and later left for the Fox Tavern, where they continued drinking. On leaving the Fox Tavern, all three men climbed over a fence into the railway sidings and broke into a covered wagon, stealing some of the contents; it was while they were breaking into another that they were disturbed by DS Kidd and DC Osbourne and, after the ensuing struggle, it was the Fox Tavern that they had returned to. It was alleged that Halliwell had said to the others, 'I stabbed him [Kidd] many times.' He also said that he thought his victim would not survive the stabbings and then left the Fox Tavern and spent the night in a boat on the nearby canal.

Further evidence against the men came out in court. The daughter of Kearsley recalled her father saying to his wife that his half-brother, Winstanley, had stabbed a policeman in the face and neck. The police surgeon gave evidence that, on examining the men, Winstanley was found to have bruises and scrapes on him that were at least two or three days old, and were consistent with DC Kidd's injuries. The newspapers covered the case with great interest, especially when the evidence presented at the hearing was sufficient for the Magistrates to commit Kearsley and Winstanley to the Liverpool Assizes. Halliwell was also committed to appear at the assizes but charged with unlawful wounding only.

There was another victim in the case, Kidd's wife. She was left with seven children and no means of support, as Kidd had left her unprovided for. The Mayor of Salford opened an appeal fund and solicited public subscriptions so that Kidd's widow could be given some means of support at this difficult time. The public came forward with generous donations and the appeal fund was a success.

In the November, while the three men were awaiting their trial, a workman was playing cards with some friends in a field between the LNWR and London & Yorkshire Railway and found a penknife that he handed to a newspaper reporter, who gave it to the local police. The police surgeon examined the knife and concluded that it was the same knife that had been used in the attack on Kidd, the damming piece of evidence being a notch in the blade that matched a wound on Kidd's body.

The trial of the three men duly took place at the Liverpool Assizes in front of Mr Justice Henn Collins. Halliwell's mental state had worsened and he was hysterical throughout the hearing, with his evidence becoming suspect, so much so that the judge directed the jury not to place too much credence on it. In his summing up, his lordship said that DS Kidd had met his death from nine wounds inflicted by a sharp instrument and that there was no reason to doubt that Kearsley and Winstanley were there. Again, he warned the jury about Halliwell's evidence and to treat it 'with the greatest possible caution'. He advised the jury on a point of law regarding the right of any member of the public to arrest a person or persons found in the act of committing a felony. If the person arrested used such violence as to cause the death of the person making the arrest, then it was murder and nothing less. The summing up was short and to the point and the jury returned a verdict of guilty without having to leave the court to deliberate. Both Kearsley and Winstanley were sentenced to death; Halliwell was discharged of the count of unlawful wounding as there was insufficient evidence.

The newspapers, who had been following the case, made their point of view about the crime and sentences quite clear. Halliwell came in for some criticism as he had become a star witness for the Crown. *The Manchester Courier* wrote:

Melancholy and mean are the details of the tragedy. It is above all things satisfactory that the culprits have been apprehended and brought to justice. Policemen and detectives, as the representatives of law and order, must be supported in carrying out their duties at all costs. Their lot is not a particularly happy one at any time but it would become intolerable if the breakers of the law could molest them with impunity.

The Liverpool Mercury was more severe in its comments:

Not one particle of sympathy can be extended to miscreants of this character who, to save the consequences of petty larceny, do not shrink from sacrificing human life.

The Liverpool Echo summed the whole matter up in its commentary:

'There yet remains the appeal to the prerogative of mercy, but in the special circumstances of the case, the murdered man having been a Policeman in the execution of his duty, it would be unwise to hold out any sanguine hope of respite.'

Kearsley appealed against his sentence of death on the grounds that he played a less prominent part in the crime and this resulted in his sentence being reduced to twenty years' penal servitude. Winstanley was the only man of the three who was executed and, before he was hanged, it is reported that he said, 'I would rather meet what I have to meet tomorrow than serve twenty years' penal servitude'. Following the execution, a large movement was set up to raise funds for the families of Kearsley and Winstanley, with the Wigan Brass Band leading a procession aimed at soliciting contributions to the fund. It appeared there was more local sympathy for the murderers of Robert Kidd than for the officer himself.

The Murder of Detective Thomas Hibbs

Thomas Hibbs was born in 1878 and, when he reached the age of twenty-one, joined the London & North Western Railway Police. No doubt, as he had just got married, he had decided to take up a steady career to support his wife and, subsequently, the two daughters they had in the next couple of years. He was a diligent young man who worked hard in the police force and was made detective by 1901 and then stationed at Birmingham, with an increase in salary that was certainly welcomed.

Over a period of time throughout 1901, the coal merchants' sidings at Curzon Street, Birmingham had been the target of large-scale thefts of coal; not just small amounts but sacks of the stuff. Needless to say, the coal merchants were unhappy that the thieving had gone unchecked and the order came down for officers of the detective branch to do something about it. Observations were mounted by the railway police but they were unable to catch anyone in the act, leading to the assumption that they were up against either professionals or lucky thieves. What the police needed was a stroke of luck to reverse the trend and this proved to be just a matter of waiting.

On the night of 10 August 1901, Detective Hibbs was on duty, patrolling in and around the Curzon Street goods depot. He knew the area well and, being aware of the danger of being on his own, put his faith in his truncheon and whistle, hoping that any blast from the latter would quickly bring assistance. He was walking near the depot when his attention was drawn by scraping noises and voices; he hurried around to the depot entrance to see three men dragging sacks of coal through the gates. Hibbs confronted the men, shouting to them, which resulted in them promptly leaving the coal sacks where they were and running for all they were worth, with Hibbs close behind them.

The men ran from Curzon Street into Fazeley Street and along the canal path, with Hibbs gaining on them. Suddenly, they turned around and faced him and it became apparent to them that Hibbs was on his own. Hibbs, now realising he was outnumbered, drew his truncheon to defend himself but, before he had time to blow his whistle, he was set upon by the three men in a vicious manner. He had no time use his truncheon as one of the men had grabbed it from him, so he lashed out and put up a good fight but was hit hard on the back of the head, which resulted in him being knocked out. Not content with leaving Hibbs where he was, unconscious on the canal path, the men picked him up and threw him into the canal where he subsequently drowned.

James Lea, an itinerant bone gatherer, usually took a bath in the canal most nights at 8 p.m. but, on this particular night, he had the fright of his life. He jumped into the canal at the junction of the Birmingham Canal and Birmingham & Warwick Canal and landed on top of Hibbs' body. After he raised the alarm, the Birmingham City Police attended the scene and began a furious and organised investigation, throughout the local area, to find the killers of their colleague. They were later joined by the officers of the LNWR Police, led by Superintendent Elijah Copping, the officer in charge in the investigation into the murder of Detective Sergeant Robert Kidd in 1895. During the initial search, pieces of coal were found on the footpath near to where Hibbs was discovered, and the following day the canal was dragged and a half sack of coal and Hibbs' handcuffs were pulled out; his truncheon was found floating in the water, just under a nearby tunnel. The police investigation was hampered by the fact that there were no witnesses to the crime. An appeal was made to the public, with the result that information came forward, statements were taken and the focus of the enquiry began to centre on Frank Parslow, Charles Webb and William Billingsley. Frank Parslow was a twenty-four-year-old, unemployed coach painter, Charles Webb was twenty-one years old and worked as a brass caster's labourer; both said they knew each other but had ceased to be friends some time ago. Billingsley was a labourer and lived locally; the focus of the enquiry, however, centred on Parslow and Webb and both made statements to the police.

There appeared to be some confusion surrounding the incident and much of the evidence that was collated by the Birmingham City Police was either indirect or circumstantial and would not stand up in court, which led them to conclude that no charges could be brought against the three men. Some witnesses had also been threatened and either withdrew their statements or confused their evidence. The investigating officers suspected that Parslow, Webb and Billingsley had knowledge of, or had committed, the murder and each had made statements implicating one other. Billingsley's statement included the admission that none of them meant any harm to Detective Hibbs and, in the beginning, it had been a lark. There was no doubt that the men had been caught stealing bags of coal and, as Hibbs was alone, they had the advantage over him. Even the recovery of a coal bag at Parslow's house, and an inadequate explanation as to why this was there, was not enough for the police to proceed further.

Curzon Street station entrance.

The canal path leading to where Detective Thomas Hibbs was murdered.

Junction of the Birmingham Canal and Birmingham & Warwick Canal, where the body of Detective Hibbs was found.

Superintendent Elijah Copping (front row, second from left). Photograph dated 1897.

The inquest at the coroners' court returned a verdict of 'wilful murder by persons unknown', which led the LNWR to put up a reward of £100 for information leading to the arrest and prosecution of these persons unknown.

The LNWR Police were not happy about the decision of the BCP to drop charges, and were not convinced by their claims that it was the availability of circumstantial evidence only which led to this. They began a review of the evidence but again, like their counterparts from Birmingham, found that it was mainly circumstantial. However, they still felt unable to understand why charges should not be brought and the evidence, such as it was, be presented to a jury for a verdict. They decided to take the case to court and charged all three men with the murder of Detective Hibbs. On 6 September 1901, Parslow, Webb and Billingsley appeared in court for committal to trial; the men's solicitor made a good case, citing insubstantial evidence, which resulted in them being dismissed on the grounds of insufficient evidence.

On 10 August, the funeral of Thomas Hibbs took place at St Mary the Virgin Church and he was buried in Colton Cemetery. Hibbs's is widow and children were joined by officers of the LNWR Police and BCP. At the bottom of the burial register, the Reverend Frederick Parker, who officiated at the service, wrote, 'Found dead in the canal at Birmingham station with marks of violence. He was a detective with the LNWR service, murdered in the execution of his duty'. To this day the murder of Detective Thomas Hibbs remains unsolved.

2

Robbery and Theft

Since the time that railways first began to carry passengers, goods and valuable cargos, they have been a magnet to the criminal fraternity, who saw them as an easy target from which to either rob or steal. It was the job of the railway police then, as it still is today, to prevent such felonious activities and to apprehend and bring to justice those criminals who thought they could plunder the railways with contempt. The following cases are just but a tiny fraction of the various crimes of this type that have been planned and committed on the railways throughout the decades.

Robbery

The Great Western Railway Robberies of 1849

The conveyance of Her Majesty's Royal Mail was considered one of the highest accolades that any railway company could have bestowed on it, demonstrating the trust and respectability with which it was viewed. The Great Western Railway prided itself on meriting this trust and, as a consequence, endeavoured to run an efficient, secure and safe contract with regard to the transportation of the Royal Mail. Until 1849, the GWR had no reason to suspect that their security was anything but tight; however, this was soon to change.

Harry Poole was employed by the GWR as a train guard and went about his work almost unnoticed. He came from a respectable family in Taunton and was married to a woman who, reputably, had been in the service of the Duchess of Sutherland. In March 1848, he was accused of theft and, although nothing was actually proved, was unable to explain the circumstances of the allegation to any degree of satisfaction and was dismissed with a questionable character. Shortly afterwards, he appeared to come into some wealth and he and his wife began to live in style in a house that was richly furnished. He was also involved in a money-lending business that became very lucrative and was thus able to sustain his sudden, lavish lifestyle. However, this was not enough for Poole, who began to think about ways of making easy money, his thoughts moving towards the mail trains that ran on the GWR, where his inside knowledge could be of some use.

Poole needed an accomplice for what he was planning and fell in with a man called Edward Nightingale, who was a horse dealer by trade in Hoxton, London, but had connections in Exeter. Nightingale was known to the police in London and his late father had been a convicted mail robber; he seemed just the partner Poole needed. Meeting on a regular basis, at the White Hart Inn at Taunton, over the next few months, the two men began to plan the robbery in detail. As Poole was known to many who worked on the GWR, he travelled up and down the railway in various disguises to see if they were effective. There was one occasion in particular where he was lucky to escape discovery; he was dressed as a labourer and was found in the area of a locked railway carriage that contained parcels. However, little suspicion was aroused as he gave a plausible reason for his being in a 'restricted' area. The plan also required agility, courage and a place to hide the contents of the mail bags once they had pilfered them. By December, everything was organised and planned for 1 January 1849.

Poole and Nightingale, disguised with false moustaches and clothing not previously worn on the trial runs, went to Starcross station, just a few miles away from Exeter, and bought two First Class, one-way tickets to Bristol, where they waited for the 6.35 p.m. Paddington – Plymouth train to arrive. This consisted of six First and Second Class carriages, a Post Office sorting van and a Post Office tender; this tender, which held the mail sacks, was the objective of the crime. When the train arrived, they boarded and settled down in a compartment in the First Class carriage next to the Post Office tender. From his previous knowledge, Poole knew the guard would join the sorters in the sorting van once they were at Exeter, leaving the tender with the mail bags unoccupied until it reached Bristol. This period was the window of opportunity that Poole and Nightingale were going to take advantage of.

The train arrived at Exeter at 9 p.m. and the men observed more mail bags being placed into the mail tender and, by feigning sleep, they ensured no one entered their compartment. The train departed on the non-stop journey to Bristol, leaving over an hour for Poole and Nightingale to put their plan into action. As the train sped through the countryside, the men opened the external carriage door and moved carefully along the carriage running board towards the tender. Poole, who was leading, took out a jemmy, wrenched the door padlock open and climbed in. Not worrying about any noise they would make due to the sound of the train, they systematically opened the mail bags and other bags containing valuables, ripping open the paper and placing the contents into two sacks they had brought with them. Keeping an eye on the time, as the train slowed on its approach to Bristol, they climbed back onto the running boards and jumped down into a field with

A railway carriage showing running boards alongside that Harry Poole and Edward Nightingale would have used.

The site where the Talbot Inn, Bristol once stood.

The original entrance to Bristol railway station.

their sacks, then made their way to Bristol on foot. When the train arrived at Bristol, the tender door was opened to reveal the robbed mail bags and the mess left behind. The police were informed and an investigation began.

When Poole and Nightingale reached Bristol, they hid the sacks in a safe place and went to the Talbot Inn, in Bath Street, to drink to their success; they had netted a haul of £150,000. The two men had already planned a second such robbery for the same night, to take place on the train to Plymouth, and left the inn to return to Bristol station at 1 a.m. The booking office was not yet open and another man, Mr Lee, a retired tradesman, was already standing there, waiting. Poole moved into the shadows while Nightingale tried the door to the booking office. Mr Lee remarked to Nightingale that the train appeared to be late but this comment was ignored and he was a little annoyed by the rudeness of Nightingale. Being a curious sort of man, Mr Lee decided to keep an eye on them; there was something about the two men that he was not happy about.

The train for Exeter arrived and the booking office opened, so Poole and Nightingale purchased First Class tickets and moved down to the end of the platform where it was dark but, just as the train was about to leave, they rushed towards a First Class compartment. A very helpful guard held the door open but, to their dismay, they saw it was occupied and hurried away to find an empty, First Class compartment, nearer the Post Office tender. Mr Lee, who was boarding the train, observed these actions, which made him even more curious and, although not really near enough to them, he tried to keep watch. Once again, Poole and Nightingale made their way to the Post Office tender, in the same way as before, and carried out this second robbery, then returned to their compartment.

When the train stopped at Bridgewater, Mr Lee passed his suspicions onto the station staff and, being aware of the first robbery, they informed the police who arrived quickly. They went to the compartment, where the blinds were drawn and Poole and Nightingale were seated. An examination of the compartment revealed a shawl under the seats containing registered envelopes, packages of valuables, false moustaches, a hook, string, candles and sealing wax. When questioned, both men denied knowing each other, with Nightingale trying to impress upon the police that he was a respectable businessman. They were arrested on suspicion of robbery and, while they were being taken away, a guard recognised Poole through the disguise he was wearing and was able to name him. Although the police were convinced that Poole and Nightingale had committed the first robbery, there was insufficient evidence to charge them. They were, however, charged with the second robbery on the Down train, the proceeds of which amounted to £4,000.

Poole and Nightingale appeared at the Exeter Assizes before Lord Justice Denman and pleaded not guilty to the charge. The prosecution produced witnesses who gave evidence that placed the defendants at the scene of the crime and at the Talbot Inn, enabling them to put forward the possibility that they had also committed the first robbery. In their defence, it was stated that it was impossible to make such a daring robbery by walking along a running board with the train travelling up to 50 miles an hour. After a two-hour speech by the defence barrister, the jury were sent out and, thirty minutes later, returned a verdict of guilty.

Before passing sentence, Lord Justice Denman addressed the defendants saying:

The evidence is so strong and overpowering that to have said you were not guilty would have been inviting others to commit similar crimes. What can one think when a discharged guard, who comes to Exeter with no apparent motive, meets another man with no honest calling, goes to Starcross and starts to Bristol, returns by the next train, comes and conceals himself, and tells a false story? The mere fact of your being present with all that knowledge and so conducting yourself, and the disappearance of the letters, would be strong enough to show that you two were the men, and you Poole, with your evident activity and skill, concealment, disguise and falsehood, bear the strongest evidence of guilt; you must be transported for fifteen years.

After all the planning, daring and risks taken in committing these two robberies, Poole and Nightingale did not have the chance to enjoy the total proceeds of £154,000. However, the punishment received for these robberies did not deter others from, in the future, attempting similar thefts from mail carrying trains, despite Lord Justice Denman's closing remarks.

The Great Gold Robbery of 1885

The transportation of gold bullion on the railways was a common practice and subject to the most rigorous security precautions. The procedures were such that no attempt to tamper with or steal the boxes had ever been made. However, on the evening of 15 May 1885, this was all about to change.

Three boxes of gold bullion were to be transported from London, via Folkestone, to Boulogne and then on to Paris. At the premises of Chaplin & Co., the couriers who regularly transported such loads, the three boxes of bullion were bound with iron hoops and then weighed and entered on the manifest. John Chaplain, the driver of the security wagon, delivered the boxes to the offices of the South Eastern Railway Company at London Bridge station. On arrival at London Bridge, the boxes were taken to the station master's office, where they were weighed and signed for by the clerk on duty. From there, the boxes were taken to the railway superintendent's office, where a senior clerk placed the boxes into two specially designed travelling safes. These safes were made of iron and were secured by Chubb locks. The keys to the safes were entrusted to specially selected staff in London and Folkestone and to the captain of the cross-channel steamer that was taking the bullion to France. In accordance with general practice, the boxes were placed in the guard's van of the night mail train. At each stage of the journey, the boxes were weighed and details entered on the manifest and then signed for.

All went well until the precious cargo reached Boulogne and the boxes were weighed there. One of them was found to weigh 40 lbs less than it had in London. The other two were found to be heavier than when they left London. All the boxes were taken intact to Paris where they were opened and it was discovered that they contained lead shot, which had been substituted for the gold. The news of this sensational crime soon became public knowledge and *The Times* reported the crime in their edition of 21 May, saying:

> A serious robbery is stated to have been committed in the transmission of specie to Paris, boxes having been opened and lead substituted for gold. It is believed to have happened at Folkestone, and the amount taken is said to be 12,000 or 14,000 £...

When the news of the robbery reached London, Detective Sergeants Smith and Thornton of Scotland Yard were assigned to the case and travelled to Paris. Fearing legal action from the bullion owners, SER asked for their solicitor, Mr Rees, to join the investigation and so protect their interests; the team was later joined by Detective Williams, also from Scotland Yard. Despite their thorough investigation, no real and tangible clues emerged other than that the lead shot was of British manufacture. All the railway staff who were involved in the process of transporting the bullion were interviewed and made statements. Nothing seemed to lead to the crime having taken place on the journey from London Bridge to Folkestone so it was considered that the crime must have occurred in France. A substantial reward was offered for information and all leads were investigated fully, but nothing of real significance emerged and the investigation went on for months without any success. It was over a year later that a breakthrough emerged.

At the end of 1856, a young woman named Fanny Bolam Kay went to the general manager's office at London Bridge to announce that she had some information about the robbery and was seen by Mr Rees. During the interview, Kay said that she had been living with a man called Edward Agar and, about three months after the robbery, he had been arrested and sentenced to imprisonment for uttering a forged cheque. When he was arrested, Agar gave the sum of £3,000 to a friend and asked him to look after Fanny. However, the friend treated her extremely badly so she decided to spill the beans. Rees found out that Agar was serving his sentence on a prison hulk at Portland and decided to interview him. He was a professional criminal and was known in America and England; he was very intelligent, a good organiser, shrewd and, while a criminal, had a code of conduct. When he was told of Fanny Kay's treatment by his trusted friend, it was enough for Agar to admit he was the organiser of the robbery and tell Rees the whole story that was recounted in the subsequent trial.

On 13 January 1857, three men appeared at the Old Bailey before Mr Baron Martin and Mr Justice Willes, charged with their part in the gold robbery. William Pierce, aged forty, was a grocer; James Burgess, a railway guard aged thirty-five, and William George Tester, a ticket collector aged twenty-six – both worked for the SER Company. Edward Agar had turned Queen's evidence and appeared as the main witness for the prosecution. Pierce had been a ticket printer with the railway but was dismissed in 1850. Burgess had worked with SER for thirteen years. Tester had been, at the time of the robbery, a clerk in the office of the SER traffic superintendent's office and privy to movements of gold bullion and other valuables on the railway. After the robbery he applied for, and obtained, the position of general manager of the Swedish Railways and had been given a glowing reference from the SER. During the trial, the full story of the robbery unfolded.

Agar knew Pierce well and it was Pierce, in May 1854, who suggested that they could plan a robbery to relieve the railways of some of the gold bullion that was carried between London and Folkestone on a regular basis. Agar felt that the risk would be too great and, at any rate, it would be too difficult to carry it off. However, Pierce said that he could get impressions of the keys for the safes; Agar was now very interested and the two decided to make plans to carry out a robbery. Later that month, both men went to Folkestone and, for a week, studied the layout of Folkestone station, the arrival of the bullion trains and the procedures for transferring the safes from the trains to the booking office and, with other details noted, they had a clear picture of all aspects of the operation. However, their close interest and hanging about the station had aroused the suspicion of the SER Police, who thought they may be pickpockets; Agar and Pierce curtailed their observations and returned to London.

The question of obtaining impressions of the safe keys was the next stage in the plan. Agar found out where the keys were kept but was doubtful they could be obtained. Pierce knew a man named Tester who could get possession of them and so approached him. As Tester was about to attempt to obtain the keys, one of them was lost and the locks on the safes had to be changed. It was about two months before Tester could get access to the new set in order for an impression to be made. Agar asked for the keys, as he wanted a First Class job done and he knew just the person who could do this. The safes had two further Chubb locks and Agar needed an impression of these keys as well, in order to open them – but how? Agar thought of a plan that involved sending a box of bullion, of £200, to Folkestone and then collecting it himself under the alias of C. E. Archer, c/o Mr Ledger or Mr Chapman. Ledger and Chapman were the two clerks at Folkestone station. In October 1854, the box was sent to Folkestone and Agar duly appeared to collect it, noting that Chapman took the keys to the safe from a cupboard drawer. Later that month, both Agar and Pierce went to Folkestone and waited until the two clerks were called from the office, to the boat train. They entered the office, made an impression of the keys and left. Agar now had the means to open the safes, but being a professional, he travelled to Boulogne and gathered information on how the transfer of the safes was handled at that end. Nothing was going to be taken to chance after nearly a year of planning. This was going to be a one-off.

Burgess was now brought into the plan and, following much discussion, it was decided not to go ahead until a substantial amount of bullion was to be moved and, furthermore, the amount should be no less that £12,000 and weighing no more than 2 cwt. They purchased this weight of lead shot and made 8 and 4 lb blocks from it, and also bought a number of carpet bags in which to carry these blocks. In anticipation of committing the robbery, the men met for several nights at the pre-arranged rendezvous until finally, on 15 May 1855, Tester tipped them off – the 8.30 p.m. train was carrying a substantial bullion cargo.

Agar and Pierce, who wore a wig and false whiskers to disguise himself, took a cab to London Bridge station and handed their carpet bags to a porter who, in turn, handed them to Burgess, the guard on the train, who placed them in his van. Pierce then entered a First Class compartment on the train and, as it began to move off, Agar jumped into Burgess's van without being seen. Agar unlocked a safe with the keys that had been made, then, with a mallet and chisel he was carrying, knocked off the metal bands around one of the bullion boxes. Taking out the gold bars, he

One of the original bullion boxes with the sack of lead inside left by Edward Agar and William Pierce.

replaced them with the blocks of lead shot, put back the iron bands and nails and resealed the boxes with sealing wax before relocking the safe. Agar had completed his task as the train arrived at Redhill station.

It had previously been agreed that Burgess would take the carpet bag containing the bullion when the train reached Redhill. While the train was stationary, Pierce left his compartment and entered Burgess's van to join Agar. Between them, they opened another safe and, in the same way as before, removed the bullion from the boxes and substituted the lead shot blocks. The boxes were put back in the same positions they were placed in at London Bridge, and the safe secured. The van was then swept clean and all evidence of the crime removed. Agar and Pierce remained in the van and got off at the station before Folkestone, then re-boarded into a Third Class carriage. When the train arrived at Folkestone, they alighted onto the platform and saw the safes being removed without any hint of trouble, then walked down the platform and entered a First Class compartment, before travelling on to Dover. At Dover, as they collected their carpet bags from Burgess's van, a porter insisted in carrying Agar's bag, causing a heart-stopping moment, but it went without further event. On leaving the station, Agar went to the pier and threw the mallet and chisel and other items into the sea, then returned to the station and travelled with Pierce back to London.

Once there, they met up with Tester and went to Cambridge Villas in Shepherd's Bush, where Agar was living at the time, and the bullion was melted down and divided up. After a suitable time, some of the gold was sold and the proceeds shared out. The remainder of the bullion was buried in the pantry of Pierce's house. Agar, unfortunately for them all as it turned out, was later arrested, charged and imprisoned for the uttering of the forged cheque.

Following the evidence of Agar and other witnesses, the jury were sent out to deliberate and come back with a verdict. All were found to be guilty of the charges against them. Burgess and Tester were sentenced to transportation for fourteen years. Pierce was convicted on simple larceny only and received two years' imprisonment, with the twelfth and twenty-fourth months to be spent in solitary confinement.

Reign of Terror

Between May 1982 and May 1983, a series of thefts, totalling fourteen robberies and three burglaries, were carried out on booking offices, mainly in the Merseyside area but also in South Yorkshire, Greater Manchester and the West Midlands. In each crime, one of the following methods was employed: the use of duplicate keys to the booking offices, posing as British Transport Police officers or posing as railway personnel. The alarming feature of six of these robberies was the fact that the criminals carried firearms and threats to use them were made to the booking office clerks if they did not do as they were ordered. The effect of this treatment was catastrophic for many of the clerks, who went on to suffer from what is today known to be post-traumatic stress disorder. The three burglaries committed at Kirby Railway station in Merseyside were carried out using duplicate keys. One set was obtained from an unsuspecting off-duty clerk who worked at the railway station; he was visited at home by a bogus railway worker who told him that he had been sent by the area manager to collect the keys. In total, the gang responsible for these crimes netted £18,249.

British Transport Police detectives liaised with officers from the Merseyside Police Serious Crimes Squad in order to catch the gang responsible for these thefts. Fingerprints were lifted from the scene of the crimes and checks made through the Merseyside Police Fingerprint Department in order to try and identify members of the gang. A press conference was held and full details of the crimes were published. Following a representation from the BTP, British Rail offered a £1,000 reward for information leading to the arrest and conviction of the offenders; this reward was to pay dividends a few days later.

A detective sergeant at Kirby police station was contacted by an informant who was tempted by the prospect of receiving £1,000. The DS and a detective constable of the Serious Crimes Squad met the informant, who told them that the gang comprised of three men; one was called John Edward Grannell, but he only knew the first names of other two, Andy and Des, and that they worked for the railway. CID officers at Merseyside Police were able to trace the two men – Andy was Andrew James Adlen, employed at Merseyrail, and Des was Desmond John Green, who worked for British Rail as a guard based in the Merseyside area. A conference was arranged between the two police forces and a surveillance operation organised under the command of two detective inspectors, one from each force. The operation was to take place during the last weekend of May, with officers from both forces taking part. In the meantime, with the knowledge of the suspects' identities, further checks were made that revealed that Grannell and Green were known to police and, in addition, their fingerprints were found at two locations, Moston and Garston, where robberies had taken place.

With this new information, the surveillance operation was called off and a revised plan was made to arrest all three men, at the same time, on 26 May 1983. This was a success and they were all taken to Walton Lane police station where, over the next forty-eight hours, they were interviewed several times. All three later elected to make statements confessing their involvement in the robberies and burglaries. Grannell admitted to twenty-four offences, Green to twenty-seven, including the burglaries at Kirby railway station, and Adlen admitted to two offences. They were charged and remanded in custody, pending trial by the South Sefton Magistrates' Court.

On 1 August 1983, they appeared at Liverpool Crown Court, before His Honour Judge Patterson. Grannell pleaded guilty to two counts of robbery and one of possessing a firearm and asked for twenty-one other offences to be taken into account. He was sentenced to ten years' imprisonment on all counts, to run concurrently. Green also pleaded guilty to the same offences with twenty-four other offences to be taken into account and received the same sentence as Grannell. Adlen pleaded guilty to two accounts of robbery and possessing a firearm, with one other offence to be taken into consideration. He received a four-year prison sentence. The judge remarked that the men had embarked on a reign of terror against railway workers who worked alone in booking offices across several counties. The convictions were the end result of a successful joint police operation between the British Transport Police and the Merseyside Police Serious Crimes Squad.

Theft

Not a Bad Day's Work

The popularity of the Metropolitan Railway Company's underground railway in London, which was opened in 1863, meant that, during the course of the day, thousands of passengers were thrown together in crowded carriages and platforms. The Metropolitan Railway Police had the task of policing the underground railway and ensuring that any illegal activity was kept in check. The criminal fraternity in London were quick to realise that this mass of travelling public would be easy prey for them to practise their art of pickpocketing on. The chances of being caught were very low and the possibility of making a good living was high.

Detective Inspector Hitchings of the MRP was well trained, both in the observation of pickpockets and in catching them in the act. In July 1876, Hitchings was carrying out this duty with his team at the Edgware Road underground station, an unfortunate turn of events for two groups of known pickpockets.

On one of the platforms, Hitchings happened to see two female pickpockets, familiar to the police, making their way through the crowded platform. He followed them discreetly, observing them working together to steal a purse and keys from a female passenger's bag without her having any idea. He then saw one of the women steal a purse from another female passenger. With assistance from his team, he arrested them both while another officer spoke to the victim who had just had her purse stolen and obtained her details. The two pickpockets, identified as Jane Bowen, forty, and Ann Coyne, thirty-eight, both married, were taken to the local police station and charged with the theft of a purse and two keys from a female unknown and the further theft of a purse and £1 7s 6d from Miss Louisa Cogger of Gloucester House, Westbourne Park.

Returning to Edgware Road station, Hitchings and his team continued their observations on the crowded station once again. Hitchings was quick to notice a man and woman working together to successfully relieve a man of his pocket watch as he was boarding a waiting train. Hitchings moved swiftly and, with assistance, arrested them. The two were identified as George Wilson, thirty-six, a commercial traveller and his wife Emma Wilson, also thirty-six. Both were taken to the police station and charged with theft of a pocket watch from a person unknown.

The two teams of pickpockets eventually appeared at the Middlesex Sessions in front of an assistant judge, the equivalent of a recorder in today's judiciary. The two teams appeared separately, but all those charged pleaded not guilty. DI Hitchings gave his evidence and provided enough proof, in both cases, for the jury to return a verdict of guilty on the prisoners. Jane Bowen was sentenced to nine months' imprisonment and Ann Coyne received six months, with both sentences being subject to hard labour. George Wilson, who had a long criminal record, was sentenced to eight years' penal servitude, while his wife was sentenced to four months' imprisonment.

For Hitchings, that day in July proved to be a very good day's work; two teams of professional pickpockets were arrested, later convicted and sentenced to long spells in prison, keeping them off the underground railway for some while.

The Case of the Non-Alcoholic Screwdriver

Dining cars were a regular feature on many long-distance train routes from the time that railways first began to operate. These dining cars not only provided food but also drinks, including alcohol. The range of drinks was numerous, varied and valuable and any stock stored on board was particularly vulnerable when the dining cars were kept in the sidings overnight.

During the winter of 1949, a number of dining cars on the London to South Wales trains were broken into and large amounts of beer, spirits and wines were stolen. In each case, the method was the same; the sliding door to the working and store area had been forced with an implement and the interior ransacked. The last raid was made on the night of 20 January 1949, and the same *modus operandi* was used as in previous raids; however, the perpetrators, no doubt feeling complacent because they had not been caught, got careless. The scene was examined by Western Railway Police detectives from Swansea, in liaison with Swansea Borough Police detectives. They noticed, during their crime scene examination of the dining car, that a tea tin had been moved from its original position. As a matter of routine, the tin was dusted for prints and a clear one was found of a left-hand little finger. The dining car staff agreed to have their fingerprints taken for elimination purposes and were subsequently ruled out of the enquiry. This indicated that the break-ins were probably the work of someone outside, most likely a local. The print was sent to Scotland Yard for further investigation but, once again, no match could be found.

This narrowed the chances of making an arrest; however the railway police inspector in charge of the case trawled through the statements and other notes on the case, and was able to fix a time frame when the dining cars were broken into. He detailed officers to keep observations at night, hoping that the offender would attempt another break in.

The wait for a breakthrough proved to be long and tedious but, after five weeks, on the night of 24 February, their patience was rewarded when they saw a man in the sidings near one of the dining cars. The detectives broke cover and approached the man to question him and, not being satisfied with his answers, they searched him and found a large screwdriver in his coat. He was arrested and taken to Swansea police station, where he was charged with being in possession of a housebreaking implement at night. The man was also questioned further about the dining car thefts but denied all knowledge and maintained his innocence. While at the station, his finger prints were taken and compared with the print from the tea tin. It was found to be a match, and this connected him with the theft on 20 January, so he was then also charged with the theft of wines and other drinks, valued at £20 3s 4d.

He was committed for trial at the Swansea Quarter Sessions and appeared there, on 6 May 1949, pleading not guilty to both charges. Evidence from the railway police investigation, including their observations, was given and this

British Transport Police officers checking a buffet car.

was supported by the verification of the fingerprint match by an inspector from Scotland Yard. Further evidence was given by a dining car conductor, who detailed the items stolen and their value. The recorder hearing the case, Mr H. Edmund Davies KC, made a witty remark at the end of the conductor's evidence by saying, 'I did not know British Railways had such an alluring array of drinks, some of which we have not heard of for some years', much to the amusement of the court and jury, who found the criminal guilty on both charges despite his insistence on being innocent. The prisoner, who did not find the quip quite so funny, had even less reason to be amused when he received a custodial sentence of nine months on each charge, to run concurrently.

A Thief Returns to the Scene of a Crime

In police circles, it has been said that, 'The criminal always makes a mistake', and, when he does, there is usually an astute officer around to spot that mistake. The following case is such an example of a criminal who slipped up and an officer who was on the ball.

In December 1950, work had commenced on repairing the roof of a London railway terminus. Following the Christmas break, work continued into the New Year without any problems until it was noticed that large amounts of lead flashing were being stolen. The railway police were informed and arrangements made for the CID to mount observations. A few days later, a detective officer was carrying out this duty on the roof of the terminus. It was a very damp and cold morning and the detective was getting cold and stiff when, just after 7 a.m. in the half-light, he saw a man on the roof carrying a sack. What, in particular, caught the officer's attention was the fact that the man was not wearing a hat or overcoat in the inclement weather. While making his way towards him, the detective was disheartened to see that the man had spotted him, clambering over the roof and making good his escape. He left behind 100 cwt of lead flashing in a sack, as well as his hat and overcoat. Unfortunately, there was nothing in the coat pockets that would give a clue as to the owner, and there the case came to a dead end.

However, a dogged detective made further enquiries and, looking through the station records on previous thefts of lead, made a connection. In June 1948, a man had been arrested and charged with the theft of lead from the same railway terminus and subsequently bound over by the magistrates' court.

The man was one James Arthur Pomroy and, although it was a long shot, the detective felt that it would be worth following up. There was no current address for the suspect, although his mother's address was on file, so she was duly visited by the investigating officers. She was shown the overcoat and hat that had been left behind and recognised the coat as the one she had brought her son for a Christmas present. She gave the officers the address where her son was now living and they decided to pay him a visit.

The following day, the officers went to the address they had been given in the guise of returning his overcoat and hat, but with the intention of questioning him about the theft of the lead. Pomroy denied any knowledge of the theft but soon found it difficult to lie when his overcoat and hat were produced by the officers, so he admitted it was he that had been on the roof on the day in question. He also admitted that he had made previous visits to the roof and had stolen lead on these occasions as well. He appeared in court, where he pleaded guilty to two charges of theft of lead and asked for three other offences to be taken into account. His repeated visits to the same terminus roof earned him a prison sentence of twelve months.

The Thief who Slipped Up

Police Constable 493, Pat O'Brien, had been in the British Transport Commission Police for twelve months, and nothing exciting or out of the ordinary had happened while he had been on duty, until 5 May 1951. The night was a filthy one – it had been raining heavily since PC O'Brien had come on duty at 10 p.m. He had been carrying out the monotonous, routine task of checking railway wagons in the goods yard at Burton-on-Trent, where he was stationed, and now, at 12.45 a.m. and thoroughly soaked through, he was making his way back to the police office to have a break and dry off. Following this, refreshed, dry and much warmer, he gave thought as to what he should do next, deciding to patrol the platforms, paying particular attention to the mail trains that had arrived during the evening.

As he walked along the platforms, he found the rear wagons of the 9.10 p.m. Bradford to Bristol train surrounded by postmen, who were finishing off loading and unloading mail bags. When they had completed their task, the train began to move out of the station and PC O'Brien noticed something move behind a pile of concrete sleepers that were stacked on the permanent way between the main line and goods yard line, near a pillar of the station bridge. Being the curious type, he decided to investigate and, when he walked further down the platform to take a closer look, he saw what seemed to be a man and some mail bags. Immediately, he jumped down off the platform onto the rails, and as he did so, the man stood up and made off under one of the bridge arches.

PC O'Brien gave chase and, in the darkness of the night, had to be guided by the noise being made by the suspect, who was attempting to scale an 8-foot-high fence. PC O'Brien scrambled under some stationary wagons in the siding and, arriving at the fence, saw the suspect running across the cattle paddock, which was extremely muddy due to the heavy rain that had been falling.

Giving chase, he gained on the man and caught up with him at a boundary fence, where he grabbed him and held onto him firmly. PC O'Brien asked him some questions and then, unhappy with the answers and with a firm grip on the suspect, he made his way back to the police office. In the meantime, two postmen, who had seen what had happened, found a couple of mailbags on the railway line and took them to the police office. The man was questioned further but would not volunteer much information and declined to make a statement. PC O'Brien decided to inform the CID and Detective Sergeant Greenwood came out to take over the case. By the time he arrived, the identity of the man had been established as Robert Aucott, a known mailbag thief, who had been arrested in 1947 for numerous daring thefts of mailbags in Cardiff and had been imprisoned for five years, only recently being released.

Greenwood questioned Aucott at length but he still refused to make a statement. During the interview, Aucott remarked that he would not have been caught if he hadn't slipped on the mud in the cattle paddock. With a typical policeman's humour, Greenwood told him that he had slipped up in more ways than one and had picked the wrong night to carry out his crime, as the fastest runner in the station police was on duty! Aucott was taken to the local police station and charged with the theft of two mail bags before being placed in a cell while Greenwood and O'Brien made further enquiries.

Returning to the office, the two policemen were handed another mailbag that had been found hidden under one of the station arches, in the cattle paddock. The bag had been cut open and it was found to contain mail addressed to Sherman Football Pools for that day's matches, and, as they were unopened, they were sent on but the bag retained. The arrest interested the Metropolitan Police, so they sent DS Peattie, who was attached to the GPO Investigation Branch. Greenwood and Peattie questioned Aucott further in regards to the offence for which he had been arrested, and in connection with the violation and theft from twenty-five mail bags in transit from Birmingham New Street to Euston in April of that year. Aucott still refused to make any statement but offered to tell the officers how he had committed the thefts in April.

He explained that he had gone to Birmingham New Street station and entered the wagon from the off-side, after the mail had been loaded. However, he was not quiet about his entry and was heard by nearby staff, who looked into the wagon but didn't notice anything strange. Aucott had hidden himself very well under the mailbags and was therefore not seen. As the train was a fast train from Birmingham to Euston, Aucott remained in the mail van and had time to go through the mailbags without interruption. He only took money and valuables from the mail and, as the train slowed down to enter Euston, he opened the van door and jumped down onto the track and made his way into London, £300 better off.

Aucott, being a man who enjoyed life, soon spent his ill-gotten gains and had to find a way of replenishing his cash reserves. Avoiding paying for a ticket, he travelled from London to Sheffield and then, on the evening of 4 May, this

A British Transport Police Commission constable checking a sealed goods wagon c. 1950.

time travelling as a fare-paying passenger, he joined the 9.10 p.m. Bradford – Bristol train. When the train stopped at Burton-on-Trent, he alighted on the off-side of the train and made his way to the mail van, where he opened the door, grabbed a bag and climbed over a fence to open it. He found it contained mail for Sherwood Pools and knew it would only be crossed postal orders and cheques and that these would be useless to him. He made his way back to the van with the intention of travelling in it, like he had done previously between Birmingham and London, and stealing what he could. However, as he opened the door, a mailbag fell out and then another fell and jammed the door. While he was struggling with the two bags, he was seen by PC O'Brien and the game was up. Ironically, these two mail bags contained high-value letters and packages.

Robert Aucott was committed to Stafford Assizes, charged with four counts of theft of the mailbags and the contents from mailbags and then set to appear before Mr Justice Sellers on 27 June. He pleaded guilty to the charges and, on passing sentence, his lordship described him as a clever and daring mailbag thief and handed him a ten-year prison sentence.

From Valuable Goods came Valuable Information

Part of a policeman's equipment are his eyes, his memory and his ability not to take everything at face value. This was ably demonstrated on a Thursday afternoon in July 1951, when a detective officer was on duty on platform ten at King's Cross station, London; he had been there since the morning rush hour and was looking forward to going home in an hour's time. At about 4.15 p.m. he happened to notice a clerk, who was employed in the parcel office, leaving the valuables office on the platform, apparently on his way home. He had noticed this particular clerk that morning; something stirred in the back of his mind so he took another look and, although not sure why, knew something was wrong. What was it that made him uneasy and bothered? Being curious, he began to think and, through his mind's eye, ran over what he was seeing. An ordinary man in a suit, carrying an attaché case, nothing wrong there – clerks often used an attaché case as they could not afford a proper briefcase. He was carrying a raincoat over his arm, quite normal behaviour, but still there was something. Then it clicked! The clerk had not been carrying a raincoat when he came to work that morning. That was it; he was carrying something he did not have earlier that day.

The detective decided to follow the clerk and made his way through the passengers towards him, but he was spotted and the man turned and ran towards the station entrance. The ensuing chase was a strenuous one for the detective, who was middle-aged, but after 80 yards he had caught up with and apprehended the thirty-six-year-old clerk. 'You know me don't you?' he asked him. 'Have you anything on you that does not belong to you?' was his next question and, to his surprise, the answer was, 'Yes, I have'. The detective took the clerk to the police office and asked him to open his attaché case, whereupon a bottle of sherry and two raincoats were found. The raincoat over his arm, on closer inspection, turning out to be two raincoats. The clerk obviously felt that the best thing to do was to co-operate with the police and he took the officer, and a colleague who had also been on a similar observation duty, to the valuables office and showed them the opened parcels from which he had stolen the goods. As the officers examined the parcels, the clerk turned around quickly and ran out onto the platform, crowded with commuters going home, and then disappeared.

Rather annoyed at the loss of their prisoner, the officers made enquiries from the railway authorities and obtained the man's address in Hackney. They became even more annoyed when, on visiting the house, it transpired that their man had not been living there for eighteen months, but they were informed that he had moved, with his family, to a new council estate in the Loughton area of Essex. Not knowing the area that well, the officers liaised with the local police and were soon knocking on the door of their runaway clerk's house. As luck would have it, they found that he had not been home and when they explained to his wife why they were there, she invited them to search the house. Luck was on their side again, as they soon found a large quantity of stolen clothing and other items.

Observations were kept on the house for the return of the clerk who, unsurprisingly, did not come home that night. The next morning, a warrant for the arrest of the clerk was issued and the search for the missing man began. It was shortly after mid day that the arresting officer, while walking back from the magistrates' court with the warrant in his pocket, spotted his clerk near King's Cross station and immediately arrested him, making sure he was not going to slip away again. The clerk made a statement in which he explained that he had always had spare money to spend on his family, but recently this had not been the case and he just wanted to maintain their standard of living. He had started stealing from the station and, because he had got away with the thefts, he continued. He was charged with four counts of theft of various items of clothing, which took place over a period of two years, amounting to a value of £232.

Two weeks later, he appeared at the magistrates' court and pleaded guilty. His solicitor pleaded for leniency and produced several character references, including one from his client's Member of Parliament, all of which alluded to his honesty and the fact that he had given valuable information to the British Transport Commission Police and was willing to help them further. The magistrate gave a serious talk to the clerk and said that he should serve a long prison sentence, however, as he had helped the police, he would serve a term of six months' imprisonment. The information passed on to the BTC police resulted in six railway porters who were working at King's Cross being arrested, charged and convicted of theft or the receiving of large quantities of stolen clothing. They were all given lengthy prison sentences.

The Case of the Wandering Tortoise

The railways have been used as a means of transporting many and varied types of goods. In this case, the goods in question were out of the ordinary – forty baskets containing 1,000 tortoises that had been ordered from North Africa by a Cambridge livestock firm. Normally, livestock would not attract the interest of railway staff but, for one man called Albert, the temptation was too great.

The baskets were delivered on 9 May 1952 to the livestock firm where, on inspection, the owner noticed that the wire securing one of the basket lids had been loosened, allowing the lid to be raised. The contents of the basket were checked and it was discovered that one tortoise was missing. It was obvious to the owner that any tortoise would not have the strength or ability to make a break for freedom in this way, and so the consignee contacted the British Transport Police at Cambridge to report the missing tortoise.

Detective Sergeant Martin and Police Constable Bunkle were assigned to the case, no doubt much to the amusement of their colleagues, and they examined the basket that had been tampered with. It became apparent that the basket lid had been forced, loosening the security wire. They next went to the goods depot and questioned the man who had checked in the baskets of tortoises. He was adamant that, as far as he was concerned, all the baskets had been secure. Other checkers were questioned, resulting in one man being singled out as having been seen hanging around the baskets earlier in the day. The checker in question, a man called Albert, was taken to one side and asked if he had taken anything home with him when he went for breakfast. 'Nothing,' he said, 'You can look round my house.' DS Martin followed this up by asking him specifically about the live tortoise. Albert gave a look of surprise and replied, 'Oh yes, someone put it in my pocket. I didn't find it until I got home. I threw it out into the garden'. It was suggested to Albert that he knew the tortoises were in the goods shed that morning and he could have easily put it back on his return, to which he replied, 'I forgot'.

Albert and the officers went to his home and a search was made, with the result that the tortoise was found in a chicken house in the garden. With all the evidence against him, Albert was cautioned and arrested for the theft of the tortoise, to which he replied, 'All right, I took it, it was crawling about the floor', a reply that did not really convince the officers. To tidy the case up, the tortoise was taken back to the livestock owner, who was able to identify it as one of those he ordered from North Africa because it was dirty and had not been deloused; if it were a 'local' tortoise it would have been clean and not in that condition.

Albert duly appeared at Cambridge Magistrates' Court on 16 May and pleaded guilty to the charge of stealing a tortoise, valued at five shillings. He was conditionally discharged, to be of good behaviour for twelve months. The hapless Albert had been working for the railways for twelve years, with a good character for all that time, but resigned before he could be dismissed – all as a result of a moment's madness.

Every Coal Sack has a Silver Lining

On the afternoon of 25 February 1953, the Maidenhead Branch of the National Provincial Bank arranged for two boxes, each containing £500 of mixed silver coin, to be sent by rail to their bank headquarters in Bishopsgate, London. The despatch of these boxes was telegraphed to Paddington station and the message duly arrived at 3.55 p.m. and was recorded in the insured book. However, owing to the lateness of the train's arrival at Paddington, the boxes could not be delivered to the bank until the following day and were deposited in the up safe in the parcel office. The usual leading porter, who worked alone in the parcel office at night, reported in sick and a replacement was found in Leading Porter W. E. Williams, who, owing to a lung infection, was on light duties but deemed suitable for the work that night.

The following morning at 4.15 a.m. a value porter was given the keys to the safe and he then loaded the two boxes of silver and other insured packages onto his barrow, and took them, via a lift, to the higher level parcel office. It was still dark at this time, but he endorsed the insured book, stating that the items in the book had been taken to the office, and then left, happy in the knowledge that he had done his job. At 6.15 a.m. a day porter opened the office and began the job of checking the insured items against the insured book entries and thus discovered that the two boxes of silver were now missing. He did not worry too much at first, as he had read the telegram that said that the boxes had been sent the previous day and assumed they had been delivered then and entered in the book by mistake. Later, after thinking about what he had discovered and the entry in the insured book, he decided to report the matter to his inspector who immediately informed the British Transport Commission Police on the station.

Detectives were put onto the case immediately and made an examination of the higher level parcel office, where they found that a wooden door, which was not in general use and normally locked, had been forced from the inside. The first action of the detectives was to visit Leading Porter Williams who was at home in bed, having worked the previous night. He denied any knowledge of the missing boxes and said that there was no bullion in his house. Enquiries continued and, as a result of these, a man called Fishlock, who lived in North West London, caught their attention. Officers called on Fishlock, whereupon he was questioned but did not convince the officers with his answers. He was taken to Paddington police station where he was interviewed in greater depth. It was not long before he told the police what he knew and made a full statement.

Fishlock said that he knew a man called Bill Williams who worked at Paddington station and who, several weeks before, had told him that there was money and other valuables for the taking there and had asked if he was up for it; Fishlock agreed to come in, on the offer made to him. Later in February, Williams and Fishlock met up and planned what they were going to do when Williams was next on night duty, which happened to be 24 February. However, their plans were cancelled until the following night as there were too many passengers and staff around for it to be safe. The next night, Fishlock met Williams at number eight platform, where a spiral staircase led to the parcel warehouse. They had enlisted the help of a bootmaker called Newman, who drove his van to the station so that the proceeds of the crime could be taken away. He was to arrive at the station at 4.30 a.m., which he duly did. Williams and Fishlock entered the warehouse via the staircase and broke open the wooden door that led into the higher level parcel office from the inside. They then took the two boxes of silver down the stairs and into Newman's waiting van. They drove to the factory where Newman worked and hid the boxes under some paper, agreeing to meet there later to divide up the contents.

With this confession from Fishlock and other related information, detectives visited Newman at his home and put it to him that he had been at Paddington station earlier that day and was involved in stealing the bullion. Newman denied everything, stating that his van had had a broken axle for weeks; the van was examined and found not to have a broken axle at all, but was a missing wheel. The detectives noticed that the grease on the axle stub and wheel was fresh, indicating that the wheel had not long been removed. Newman stuck to his story and was taken to Paddington police station for further questioning. Following this, the officers went to the factory where Newman worked and recovered one of the bullion boxes. Williams was interviewed again and the facts put to him once more, along with the evidence given by Fishlock. He admitted he was in on the crime and added that he didn't have long to live and refused to say any more.

The three men were formally arrested and charged and it was then that Newman, while being placed in a cell, told the officers he would take them to where the money was and also admit his part in the crime. Newman took the officers to a shop where he had a small business and, once there, to a back room where he opened a trap door. In the cellar, the officers recovered five coal sacks containing £258 6d.

All three appeared at the Central Criminal Court in due course, and were found guilty and sentenced to two years of imprisonment each. They all asked for thefts of parcels from Paddington station, from the January onwards, to be taken into account as well.

What a Fag Police Work can be

When a railway ganger was walking along the embankment, in November 1956, near to Frodsham in Cheshire, he was not surprised to see the usual rubbish lying around – newspapers, food wrappers, a broken umbrella, cigarette packets and tins of tobacco. He stopped suddenly and looked again; tins of Ogden's tobacco, unopened and laying on the embankment. Being an honest chap, or probably not a pipe smoker, he picked up the tins and handed them in to the nearest British Transport Commission Police office. There the matter rested until 29 December, when a number of Ogden's tobacco tins were found near to the spot where the first ones had been discovered. Seeming to be a bit more than coincidence, the local BTC Police decided to further investigate this sudden appearance of tobacco tins.

Enquiries established that it was more than probable the tins were thrown from a passenger train and this was likely to have been the 10.45 p.m. from Liverpool Lime Street to Chester, with Friday being the most likely day. Consequently, officers travelled on the 10.45 p.m. train for several Friday evenings in a row but nothing untoward happened. This prompted a more detailed look at the facts and it was noticed that there was a six-week gap between the two dates when the tobacco was found; this led to the enquiry looking into the possibility that staff were involved in the thefts. Detectives examined the working schedules of engine drivers and guards and narrowed the suspect down to a guard who manned the 9.10 p.m. train, from Liverpool Lime Street to Chester on the particular dates of interest. It transpired that in front of all these trains was a goods wagon for Cardiff, loaded with Ogden's tobacco products! With these new facts, it was decided to keep observations on the train that fitted into the previously identified six-week pattern.

The 22 March 1957 saw a detective at Liverpool Lime Street having a look inside the sawdust box in the guard's van on the 9.10 p.m. and, lo and behold, he found tins of Ogden's tobacco. He decided to delay making enquiries and instead continued to travel on the train as a passenger. When the train stopped at Chester, he went to the guard's van and opened the sawdust box but found it to be empty. Seeing the guard standing on the platform, he went up to him and identified himself, producing his warrant card. The detective asked the usual questions and received the usual answer that he, the guard, did not know anything that would help the detective with his enquiries. The officer was not at all satisfied with this and so arrested the guard on suspicion of theft and took him to the police office on the station.

Once there, the guard regained his memory and became more co-operative. He said that the tobacco was in his bag and produced the invoice that had accompanied it. He admitted taking a carton on Thursday evening and took the officer to a place in the goods yard, where an empty carton was found with the address of the intended recipient still on it. They returned to Liverpool, where the guard lived, and tobacco from the carton was recovered there with more being found when his locker at Garston Docks was searched. Returning to Chester, the guard made a statement in which he admitted stealing the tobacco and he was then charged.

Appearing at Chester Magistrates' Court, the guard pleaded guilty to two charges of stealing tobacco and asked for two further charges to be taken into account. He was sentenced to four months of imprisonment on each charge, to run concurrently, and also lost his job.

We are Watching, Always Watching!

Members of staff in Plumstead goods yard were going about their duties as usual and not taking much notice of the wider world. However, for five railway staff, their work was to be interrupted, with huge implications for both them and their families. Plumstead goods yard had several sidings and one of them, known as Polytechnic Sidings, handled all the goods wagons entering or leaving the yard. A large number of these wagons were used by the Ministry of Supply and other government departments, all based at the Royal Arsenal and Woolwich Dockyard yard. There was a designated spur road leading from the sidings, with a ministry checker to ensure that the correct wagons were sent to the correct points within the Arsenal and Dockyard.

For some considerable time, regular thefts from these government wagons were taking place and detectives from the British Transport Commission Police were given the task of investigating the thefts and arresting the criminals. The result of keeping observations on the sidings was that they uncovered other crimes, an added bonus one may say, which led to the clearing up of many unsolved cases. After many hours of observations and enquiries, the majority of which were fruitless, the officers in the case gathered sufficient evidence to make arrests.

Sidings at Plumstead goods yard.

One day in late February 1957, between 1.30 and 10.30 p.m. the officers swooped on the goods yard, questioned all available staff and searched their lockers, with the result that missing property was recovered and five members of staff, a ganger, a head shunter, two under shunters and an acting yard foreman, were arrested. It transpired that all of these men had been significantly engaged in long-term theft of government property. They all made statements blaming each other for their fall from propriety and declared that they had not done anything like this before!

The men appeared at Woolwich Magistrates' Court later that month, pleading guilty to the charges laid before them. Three men were each fined £45 or three months' imprisonment, another was fined £30 or two months' imprisonment and the fifth man was fined £10 or one month's imprisonment. It went without saying that all five men were dismissed from their employment with the railway and that this sent a warning across Plumstead goods yard.

In the Frame

Sometimes a chance observation, or being in the right place at the right time, can be a lucky break for police officers. Such was the case on 4 September 1959, when two detectives of the British Transport Commission Police, stationed at Manchester London Road station (now Manchester Piccadilly station), happened to pass the home of a railway porter who was known to them and saw him taking photographs with what looked like a new camera. On their return, they checked through the files and found a list of stolen property, reported on 18 August, which included the camera they had seen earlier that day.

The following Monday, the two officers saw the porter and told him they believed that he was in possession of a stolen camera. The porter denied the allegation, saying that he had borrowed it from his brother. The officers asked if they could see the camera and the porter took the officers to his home, where he produced the item in question. It was not the same as the one detailed on the stolen property list. The porter then invited the officers to search his home; he was either bluffing, hoping the officers would not carry it out, or he was very naïve. The officers took him up on his invitation and found a Zeiss Ikon camera, matching the description of the stolen item, in a cupboard. It had been left on a train by an Australian visitor who was meeting relatives before returning home, and had been reported by her as such. The porter admitted that he had taken this camera at a time when he had been on 'train searching' duty. He also admitted that he had taken the first camera from the empty stock of another train. By finding one camera, the officers had found another. The porter was arrested and charged, appearing before Manchester City Magistrates' Court on the following day. He pleaded guilty to two charges of 'larceny servant' and was fined a total of £5.

That evening, the same two detectives were on duty again at Manchester London Road station and received information that another porter who was on 'train searching' duties had booked in on duty at 6 p.m. but had not been seen since; the time now being 6.18 p.m. The officers went to the station chief inspector's office and asked for an announcement to be made over the station tannoy system, requesting that the porter return to the office. By 6.54 p.m. there had been no response. The officers came to the conclusion that he may have heard about the arrest of the other porter on the previous day and then gone home to dispose of any stolen property. Armed with the porter's home address, the detectives were about to leave the station when they saw him walking along the road from the direction of the city.

They stopped the porter and took him to the police office, where they asked him why he had left the station. At first, the porter replied that he had been to the post office to post a letter; then he said he had been home to give his wife some money, but he denied knowing anything about stolen property. He agreed to go back to his house with the officers and, during the journey, he admitted he had left the station to go home and hide some stolen property. When the porter and officers arrived at the house, the porter handed over a large quantity of bed linen that he had stolen from the station linen store. He was arrested and charged and appeared the following day at the magistrates' court, where he pleaded guilty to 'servant larceny' and was sentenced to one month's imprisonment.

The next day, 10 September, the officers followed up on further information that had come their way as a direct result of the arrests of the previous days. It seemed as if the station staff wanted to clear the air and dropped interesting snippets of information in the direction of the police. These suggested that a third porter engaged on 'train searching' should be asked a few questions. This they did, but the porter denied having anything to do with stolen property. He was asked if he would allow the officers to search his home, which was in fact his lodgings, and he agreed. As in the previous case, the officers found a quantity of British Railway bed linen in his rooms but the porter again strenuously said that he had nothing to do with it. The officers were not impressed by his impassioned denials and arrested him. He was bailed to appear before the magistrates' court on 9 December to answer the charge of larceny and he pleaded not guilty, instead electing to go for trial before the assize court. The case was adjourned for a week and, just before the hearing, the porter approached the detectives and, although still denying the charge of stealing, explained that he wanted to clear the matter up. He told the officers that he had been given the linen by another porter, disclosing his name. He was re-charged with receiving stolen goods to which he pleaded guilty and was fined £5.

That same evening, at 11.30 p.m. the two officers, who were no doubt feeling pleased with their work over the past few months, went to a fourth porter's home to arrest him for stealing BR bed linen, the subsequent search of his house providing further stolen property. He was arrested and charged and appeared the following day at the magistrates' court, where he pleaded guilty to larceny and had another offence taken into account. He was fined £10. This case goes to show that one simple observation, in combination with good old-fashioned police work, can lead to a whole series of crimes being unravelled and solved.

The Runaway Train

In 1962, a national rail strike took place, and engines and rolling stock were parked up in sheds and sidings throughout the country. On 3 October of that year, an extraordinary incident occurred. A railway apprentice was standing on the platform at Derby Midland station when he heard an engine approaching. Looking round, he saw, to his surprise and horror no doubt, a main-line diesel locomotive careering through the station without anyone in the cab. The train continued speeding down the line through signals set at danger, a precaution that signalmen had taken before leaving their posts to join the industrial action. When the locomotive came to a set of points, it derailed and landed on its side, causing extensive damage not only to itself but also to the surrounding rail track.

The British Transport Police at Derby immediately launched an investigation to establish what had happened. The locomotive was a 2,300 hp main-line engine, weighing 130 tons and valued at £100,000, which had been parked in the engine sheds at Derby. In order for the engine to keep travelling, the dead man's handle, a device that if not held down would stop the engine within ten seconds, must have been engaged by someone crouching low in the cab or been physically weighed down. The controls were removed to be examined for fingerprints and to establish whether or not the thief had jumped from the train as the engine left the rails; police dogs were called in to try and track his movements after leaving the scene. Consideration was given by the BTP as to whether to fingerprint thousands of rail men who worked at the Derby locomotive, carriage and wagon works, but this was discounted as impractical. Over the next two days, BTP officers interviewed railway men to establish if they knew anything. Their persistence finally paid off – during an interview, a seventeen-year-old apprentice fitter admitted to stealing the locomotive.

The youth, who was not on strike, got the idea as he was finishing work and saw six engines standing in number two shed. When all his workmates had left and the coast was clear, he put his bicycle into the cab of the locomotive and climbed in. He started the engine and drove out of the shed and onto a freight loop near Derby Midland station, heading for the Chaddesden sidings. He said that he never did more than 20 mph even though the engine was capable of 90 mph and safely crossed about twelve sets of points that were clear. As he rounded a sharp bend, he saw a signal against him and put the brakes on hard. This, coupled with the momentum of the train, caused the engine's brakes to lock and the locomotive slid across the points and toppled onto its side. As the engine fell over, the youth jumped out of the driver's seat and, when the engine came to a stop, broke a cab window, threw his bicycle out and cycled home as if nothing had happened.

The youth was charged and taken before Derby Magistrates' Court, where he pleaded guilty and was sentenced. Despite this, he was a fortunate young man indeed to have escaped from the crashed locomotive with no damage to himself or his bicycle.

The Darby and Joan Thieves

In April 1968, the British Transport Police at Heysham were involved in investigating the theft of cable from the old Morecambe – Lancaster branch line. Both CID and uniformed officers of the BTP maintained observations on the line for a long period of time without any results, so the observations were called off. A few days later, the BTP were told by the local police that information had been received about a gang of thieves who were planning to steal a substantial amount of copper cable from the branch line and there was the chance they could turn violent in order to secure the cable.

Observations were reinstated straight away at a junction box near Lancaster Green Ayre station, even though there was no indication when the theft might take place. The observations were continued for several nights, again without any results. The surveillance was called off once more as it was detracting from other police work, so arrangements were made with the Signal and Telegraph department to set up an alarm system. It was silent and consisted of an alarm that would activate if a cable was tampered with and would show as an intermittent light on a particular circuit at Lancaster (Castle) station.

On 14 May, just after midnight, the alarm was triggered and the police in Lancaster and the BTP were alerted by the switchboard operator. At this time, there was only a uniform constable on duty at Heysham. He drove to the junction box area and, carrying a torch, climbed over a fence, then drew his truncheon in anticipation of meeting the violent gang. Carefully making his way towards the junction box, he heard a noise and so switched on his torch; in the beam of light, he saw an old man holding a quantity of copper cable and, by his side, a 'blowsy' older woman. Both were standing next to severed ends of cable, near the junction box. At this point, the Lancashire Constabulary turned up with their dogs and the 'violent' gang were rounded up.

The next morning, CID officers from Heysham took over the case and established that the severing of the cable had caused extensive disruption to telephone, telegraphic and circuit systems between Morecambe, Lancaster and Heysham. The woman was released without charge but the man was charged with malicious damage and with the larceny of two yards of twenty-four pair, PVC-covered cable. He appeared at Lancaster Magistrates' Court the next day and pleaded guilty. In mitigation, he told the court that he was sixty-one years of age and had no fixed abode, with a history of criminal activity. He put his misfortune down to women and drink and the fact that his girlfriend, who was fifty-nine years old, had provided the transport to make their getaway with the cable. He was placed on probation for three years on the first offence and fined £5 for the second.

Following the revelation about the getaway transport, the officers involved in the case became worried. Had they been negligent in not searching the crime area properly and could it have contained further amounts of cable? Worried that they may have not been thorough, they asked the old man if he would take them back and show them where he had parked the vehicle. Obligingly, the man went back with the officers and, under a nearby tree, proudly showed them a very old and rusty pram! After they had taken in the shock of seeing 'the transport', the quiet of the surrounding countryside was broken by the raucous laughter of police officers who, despite the seriousness of the crime, found a funny side to the close of this case.

Not so Squeaky Clean

In October 1969, the British Transport Police at Guildford received information from a woman passenger concerning the car park at Woking station. She believed that the car parking fee she had paid, to a railwayman at the station, had been pocketed and not paid in as it should have been. Officers began an investigation and eventually interviewed and charged a railwayman with four counts of obtaining money by deception. During the routine questioning, the suspect was asked by the officers whether or not he had any stolen property at his home. He replied that he had not and invited the officers to search there, if they so wished. Needless to say, the officers did wish to and took him up on his kind offer!

Accompanied by the railwayman, they made an initial search of the house and found nothing. However, one officer decided that, before they left the house, he would have a look in the attic. The loft hatch was opened and he heaved himself up and found a treasure trove of washing powder products, neatly stacked. Initially, the railwayman expressed surprise at the discovery but, after further questioning, admitted that he had stolen the boxes of washing powder when they passed through the National Carriers depot at Woking.

Officers were of the opinion that this was not the end of the investigation, and that there were other people involved in the theft of goods at the Woking depot. Following a trail of washing powder, metaphorically speaking, they made further enquiries, which led them to one National Carriers employee and then, from there, to two more members of staff. The three employees were all arrested for the theft of washing powder and, at that point in the enquiry, the police were informed that some coalmen working in the yard at Woking were not exactly squeaky clean either. The investigating officers interviewed three coalmen and searched their homes, where soap products were found stashed away, resulting in them being arrested and charged with theft.

All seven men: one railway man, three National Carriers employees and three coalmen, appeared at Woking Magistrates' Court and pleaded guilty to the charges against them. Fines, totalling £245, were imposed and the defendants left the court with a stain on their character that no amount of soap or washing powder would be able to expunge.

The detective sergeant and the officers who investigated the case were given the dubious honour of being known collectively as 'the men who cleaned up Woking' by both their colleagues and the officers in the local force.

3

Ticket Irregularities, Forgery and Fraud

The avoidance of paying railway fares has been, and still is today, one of the most committed crimes on the railways. Each year, there are thousands of passengers who see free travel as fair game and are successful in carrying out this deception. However, there are just as many passengers who are caught and successfully prosecuted. Forgery and fraud take many forms and these crimes are fully investigated by the railway police when they come to their notice. The following cases illustrate some of the devious ways in which these offences are committed and how they have ultimately been unsuccessful.

A Fishy Business

A lesser-known fact about the railways is that, in days gone by, they owned hotels, most of them attached to main-line railway termini. These hotels came under the jurisdiction of the British Transport Commission Police, who were called in to investigate any crimes that may have been committed on the premises.

In April 1949, the BTCP were contacted by an informant, who told them that the Hotel Executive was being defrauded of about £2,000 a year through false transactions concerning the supply of fish and poultry to one of their hotels in the London area. Resulting from this information, the BTCP began an investigation that centred on a well-known and respected firm of London caterers and hotel staff. The investigation was a protracted one but ended in the successful prosecution of some of those involved.

The business of arranging with suppliers for the provision of fish and poultry to the hotel was handled by one of the catering company's managers. In league with him were members of his staff, comprising a cashier, two salesmen and a delivery man. The staff involved, from the hotel concerned, included a stores clerk and a kitchen clerk. All these were aware of the activity going on and were benefiting in some way. During the investigation, other hotel staff came under suspicion, but there was insufficient evidence to prosecute them.

The fraud was conducted in the following manner. In regard to the fish, boxes were weighed at the caterer's shop and details entered into a delivery book, with the correct description, weight and value being noted. A second delivery book was then prepared, showing an incorrect, inflated weight and value. The delivery man was given instructions by the manager to obtain a signature in the second book, provided there was no risk of the discrepancy being discovered; if there was, then he was to obtain a signature in the correct delivery book. The usual routine, when the fish was delivered, was that the kitchen clerk signed whichever book was presented to him, without question. The fish was never weighed and was sent straight away to the kitchen, where it was immediately cleaned and cut into portions. Within a short time of being delivered, all traces of the consignment being underweight were destroyed.

When the delivery man returned to the caterers, the two delivery books were handed to the cashier who examined them and destroyed the unsigned delivery note. The hotel was later sent an account, which included requests for payments for fish that had not actually been delivered. For example; payment for 75 lbs of cod was invoiced, whereas only 50 lbs of cod were actually delivered. Payment to the caterers was by cheque and these transactions occurred on a daily basis and were not queried by the customer. There was a procedure in place for spot checks on deliveries but it had become the norm to make these on a Monday, so any element of surprise was gone. However, if the day was changed, the manager of the caterers was tipped off by one of his contacts in the hotel and so only the correct delivery book would be produced.

The fraud relating to poultry was a simple one. The agreed legitimate system was that each poultry delivery would be accompanied by a delivery note in duplicate and a signature obtained. One of the notes would be retained by the hotel stores clerk and the other returned to the caterers for their records. The fraudsters operated the following scheme in order to cover up their crime. If two cases of poultry were delivered in a morning, nothing would be signed for. Later in the day, the hotel stores clerk would visit the caterers' manager and indicate by how much the weight of the delivered poultry could be increased. Then a delivery note was raised for the weight and quantity decided on, and signed for. An account would be sent to the hotel and it would again be paid for by cheque.

The question of how those involved were to receive their share of the fraudulent gains had to be addressed, as all payments were made by cheque. The manager of the caterers looked after this part of the fraud. He was authorised to purchase large amounts of fish and poultry and pay the supplier by cheque or cash. He usually paid by cash, with the money being taken from the shop cash register. The manager then calculated the inflated amount paid by cheque by the hotel for supplies. He produced a bill for an 'alleged' cash purchase of fish and poultry that covered this larger amount. The bill was passed to the cashier who withdrew the sum, in cash, from the till and the amount above the actual delivery cost was used to pay all those involved their share of the fraudulently obtained money. The fraud was quite ingenious as the 'fictitious bill' balanced the till record. The amount paid by the hotel, i.e. the inflated amount, covered the value of the purchases shown on the fictitious bill. When the accounts were audited, an overall correct balance would show and no questions would be asked.

At the end of the police investigation, four people were arrested and charged with fraud by false pretences, attempted false pretences, defalcation of accounts and larceny. Two hotel staff were dismissed by the Hotel Executive, despite the evidence not being strong enough to bring a prosecution, as they were found negligent in their duties. The average sum defrauded in total by the gang, over the period of time concerned, varied from between £20 to £40 a week, with one member of the gang receiving £15 each week and the remainder being shared among the rest. The fraudsters appeared in court and pleaded guilty, receiving sentences that ensured that they would not be able to spend any more of their ill-gotten gains for a considerable time.

Not for the Privileged

Privilege tickets are a perk for employees of the railway and allow them to travel, when off duty, at a reduced rate compared to that of the ordinary customer, so when abuse of this perk is suspected, it becomes a serious matter.

For the travelling ticket inspector on the 6.55 p.m. train from Paddington to Fishguard, one evening in early 1953, it appeared to be just another ordinary working day. He went through the train, checking passengers' tickets as usual, and eventually came to the Third Class carriages. He entered one compartment occupied by a man and two women; the man proffered three single privilege tickets from Paddington to Rosslare, all of which were stamped with the letter W, indicating that they were issued for women only. When questioned about the tickets, the man, who gave the name Howlin, said that the two women with him were his sisters. The inspector, far from happy about his interview with Howlin, wrote a report that was submitted to the British Transport Commission Police ticket fraud office at Paddington.

The police began investigating the case and established that the privilege tickets were issued by the Southern Railway Company and had been authorised against a pad of privilege travel vouchers that, at the time, had not been issued for distribution. The signature of the authorised person issuing the vouchers was T. Ashton, a superintendent in the dining car department; however, it was soon established that this was a fictitious name, as were those of the employees to whom the travel vouchers were issued.

The BTC police officer investigating the case interviewed one of the women, named Sanders, who had been travelling with Howlin. She admitted that she had approached a friend named Miller and asked him if he could obtain some cheap rail tickets for her. A few days later, he gave her three vouchers that she could use in exchange for reduced fare tickets, charging her 10s each for them. Miller was interviewed next and confirmed that what Sanders had said was true; in addition, he had seen a dining car attendant named Grice who had sold him the three vouchers for 5s each, having all been filled out. Grice was interviewed and denied that he had sold the vouchers, as it was more than his job was worth and he had not seen Miller for a long time.

The investigating officer left the matter for a few days in order to keep the men guessing about what was going to happen; he then arranged a meeting and took statements from them. He informed Miller that Mrs Sanders would be reported for obtaining the vouchers and that he would be reported for aiding and abetting. Grice was seen next and informed that he would be reported for uttering a forged document, as the signature on each voucher had been forged by him.

To prove forgery is a difficult process and, even in the 1950s, was an expensive one. However, the assistant chief of police in the London area had the foresight to set up a department supplied with infra-red photography and ultra-violet equipment. The forged documents and a specimen of Grice's handwriting were tested and compared. This examination established that the writing on the travel voucher had been done with a ballpoint pen, whereas the signature had been written with an ink pen in an attempt to make the documents look authentic. It was common practice for a junior clerk to make out the voucher with a ballpoint pen and for the authorising officer to sign approval with an ink pen. Despite all these clever efforts by Grice to make the vouchers look correct, they did not stand up to the forensic tests and handwriting comparison, and a detailed statement was prepared to support the findings.

Summonses were served on Grice, Miller and Sanders to appear at Marylebone Magistrates' Court, where only Grice was legally represented. Miller and Sanders pleaded guilty and were fined £3 and £1 10s respectively. Grice pleaded not guilty and elected to go to trial at the Central Criminal Court, returning to the magistrates' court a few weeks later for a pre-trial hearing. The BTCP solicitor presented the case, and his statement, along with the incriminating forensic evidence, made a damming case against Grice, who then changed his plea to guilty and asked for the case to be heard by the court; they fined him £7, with costs amounting to ten guineas.

This was the first case where forensic evidence of this type was used by the BTCP and one of its officers and, as such, gained a place in the history of the railway police.

Attack is the Best Form of Defence – Sometimes

On occasion, people can be too clever for their own good. This was certainly true for a lecturer at Leeds University in 1969. The gentleman concerned was the son of a Polish immigrant, who had been using the railway to attend the university for some years. He had an arrogant attitude and was well versed in being economical with the truth when necessary; the fact that he had come to the notice of the British Transport Police when he was younger may have contributed to his demeanour in the events that followed, when he once again came up against the police.

On the 3 June, the lecturer went to the ticket barrier at number seven platform at Hull railway station, one minute before the train was due to leave, and presented a First Class, three-monthly return ticket, valid between Hull and Leeds. The ticket collector noticed that the ticket bore a punch mark and drew the lecturer's attention to this fact, as it indicated the ticket could have already been used on the outward part of the journey, making it no longer valid for travel between Hull and Leeds. He claimed that he had missed the train two or three days before and had not used it for travelling and asked if the ticket was still valid. As the train was about to leave, the ticket collector allowed him through but advised the travelling ticket inspector, who was boarding the same train, about the situation. The inspector went through the train, checking passengers' tickets and eventually met up with the lecturer and queried the ticket, asking him to account for the punch-mark on it. The lecturer replied that he had to dash for a train the other morning and had missed it. On being pressed by the inspector, he added that he was on the platform and had met a friend and missed the train because he was talking to him. 'When?' the inspector asked, to which the lecturer replied, 'About three or four days ago.' Pressed further, he said, 'It was Saturday'. Now, the Saturday in question was 31 May. The lecturer then took the stance of being a maligned person and, at first, refused to give his name and address when asked. Eventually, however, he did and produced a monthly Second Class season ticket, for travel between Hull and Leeds, that had expired; he initially refused to give this up but finally ceded when pressed by the inspector. The expired season ticket bore the same date of issue as the punched, First Class return ticket, that of 29 April.

The result of this conversation was that the lecturer made a personal complaint to the acting assistant station master at Leeds, on the same day, in which he maintained his story that the ticket had been punched on the Saturday. The following day, 4 June, the lecturer saw the assistant station master and, in the presence of the acting assistant station master, when asked about purchasing the offending ticket replied, 'Three or four days earlier'. He then followed up on his defence by sending a four-page letter to the divisional manager, stating that he recollected that it was four days earlier. A police sergeant was sent to see the lecturer at his address and was greeted with a display of indignant behaviour and asked to leave the house; the lecturer was under the misapprehension that the sergeant was appearing on behalf of the railway to apologise, and felt put out when he realised this wasn't the case. He followed this up with a complaint to his solicitor, who contacted the police. When asked if he would be present at an interview between the police sergeant and his client, the reply was, 'Take your pick – apologise or issue a summons'. Taking the latter course of action, the police began to investigate the case further.

The sergeant realised that the case rested on the date that the punch mark was made, tying in with when the lecturer said he had previously intended to travel, and the actual date had not been clarified with any certainty. Despite the best efforts of the sergeant, he was unable to obtain this information. Further enquiries revealed that it could not have been Saturday 31 May, as the ticket punch that was used, identified as number '33V' with a triangular hole, was exclusively issued to a ticket collector named Barnes, who was off duty on the day in question. The sergeant reviewed the case and was concerned that the defence could allege that any one of the two, three or four days prior to the 3 June, the day of the offence, could have been the day of the lecturer's intention to travel, and so the ticket may have consequently been punched on any of these days, not just the Saturday. Furthermore, it would be in the defence's interest to allege that the actual day was Friday 30 May, the fourth day prior to the 3 June as this would be consistent with Barnes' rota. If Barnes was called to give evidence, then the defence could not fail to say it was the fourth day and this presented a dilemma for the police inspector who would be prosecuting. Should he call Barnes and give the defence the gift of realising the significance of when he could not have punched the ticket, rather than when he did? The sergeant consulted relevant case law and the 'Conditions of the carriage of Passengers and their Luggage', then wrote up his case and submitted it for consideration for the prosecution of the lecturer. A summons was duly issued and served on the lecturer to attend the Hull Magistrates' Court and answer the charge.

On the day of the hearing, the BTP was represented by a prosecuting police inspector and the defence by the lecturer's solicitor. The prosecution opened the case by stating that the ticket was not valid at the beginning of the journey on the 3 June as it was defaced. A valid ticket, produced at the barrier, allows the holder to travel on the railway and pass through onto the platform at the commencement of the journey. The ticket in question had been invalidated for further use for the particular part of the journey being made, due to it being defaced by a ticket collector's punch mark. The case for the prosecution having been outlined, the hearing continued.

Witnesses were called and examined, cross-examined and re-examined. Questions arose such as, 'What motive could there be? How could the ticket be retained at Leeds? Why did the lecturer refuse an explanation to the police sergeant when he visited? Was the lecturer not justified in asking for an apology?' The only witness not called at this stage, was Barnes. The defence called the lecturer to the stand and, typically, he assumed his maligned and arrogant tone. In his evidence, he said he was certain the day in question was Saturday 31 May and he was intending to catch the 7 a.m. train and had been talking to a friend, whom he met on the platform. Next, the defence called the friend who, under oath, substantiated the lecturer's evidence.

The case for the prosecution was not going well and the police inspector was dismayed when, on asking the court if he could call ticket collector Barnes as an expert witness, he heard the clerk reply, '*Ex Improviso*'. The clerk was referring to the fact that the court and defence should have been informed about this witness. The inspector argued that the court should hear the witness's evidence as the facts presented so far were in dispute and this information would throw further light on the case. The court agreed and Barnes took the stand and gave evidence that he was not on duty on the day in question and therefore could not have punched the ticket as suggested; without any mention of the possibility of it being Friday not Saturday. This brought the whole story told by the lecturer into question. It was a risk worth taking as, after deliberation, the court found the case against the lecturer proved. He was fined £4 for attempting to travel on an invalid ticket, £2 for travelling and also had to pay the prosecution costs of £6. The inspector and sergeant were commended on the preparation and prosecution of the case.

Just the Ticket

It was a cold morning, on 26 January 1971, and ticket collector Morris was on the early shift at Brighton station; consequently, he was not quite awake, but was alert enough to spot something unusual that caught his eye. He was examining the tickets of passengers who had alighted from the 6.03 a.m. Hove – Brighton train when a male passenger presented a three-monthly Second Class season ticket from Hove & Brighton to London, which appeared to be correct. However, he also noticed that the passenger was holding another season ticket in the opposite hand, which appeared identical to the one he had just produced. Morris was occupied with examining other passengers' tickets and called over his colleague, ticket collector Kelly, to check for him. Kelly examined both the season tickets, which looked genuine at first glance, but then noticed that they bore the same serial number, 0066, although one was dated '4 Jan 71' and valid until '04 Apr 71', while the other was dated '25 Jan 71' and valid until '25 Apr 71'. Not happy about the situation, he called the British Transport Police office on the station and a uniformed constable duly arrived.

The constable questioned the man, named Richardson, a printer and compositor who worked in London and travelled daily to Victoria station. Richardson, who realised his luck had now run out, explained that he had bought one of the tickets from a man unknown to him for £5. He could not describe the man and, furthermore, stuck to his story that he believed this ticket to be genuine. As it was so early in the morning, the officer was not in a position to check if the ticket was a forgery or not, and so he kept both tickets, took Richardson's details and made arrangements to see him later that day. After having to buy another ticket, Richardson went on his way to work in London.

Later in the morning, while at work, Richardson was visited by the constable and a CID officer from Victoria and questioned further about the season tickets. He kept to the original story that he had given to the constable earlier that day, and would not deviate from it. After some careful questioning, Richardson finally admitted forging the ticket with another printer named White, who had possession of the equipment they needed. White was summoned and he turned out his locker, which was found to contain the stamps and dies that were used and another ticket that was not up to standard.

Richardson had obtained some green card from work, identical to that used for railway season tickets. Being a good artist, he drew letters and figures in the correct type required and took them to engravers, who then made some photoelectric plates. In order to disguise their true purpose and thus allay any suspicion, the drawings were made in the guise of a calendar. The tricky part was to forge the ten lines with the wording 'BRITISH RAIL', ten times on each line, which all forms the background to the date on the season ticket. He composed a sentence reading 'Buy British Goods Only, when Shopping, says Mrs. Rail' and had them made up into type blocks of ten lines of this sentence. By taking out the words 'British' and 'Rail' from ten blocks of ten lines and then joining them together on one block to place onto the photoelectric plate, they were able to overcome the most difficult part of forging the season ticket.

The day Richardson was caught, he was carrying out a dummy run to check the accuracy of the ticket and see if it would pass muster. Unfortunately for him, the only dummy in the run was he himself. Evidence was also gathered to prove that, if this test had been successful, Richardson and White would have gone into full production and flooded the rail market with high-quality forged season tickets.

Richardson and White were arrested and charged with forgery and, in addition, Richardson was charged with uttering a forged document at Brighton station. Appearing at Clerkenwell Magistrates' Court the following day, they pleaded guilty and White was fined £100, while Richardson was fined £100 on each of the two charges laid before him.

The forged ticket was of a high standard and, if Richardson had not made the mistake of having both tickets on show and without the sharp-eyed observation of ticket collector Morris, this crime would have gone undetected. If you are wondering which season ticket was genuine, it was the one dated '4 Jan 71'.

In for a Penny, in for a Pound

One fine day in August 1973, Christopher Graham wanted to travel from Blackpool to Leicester, but he had a problem – he had no money to purchase a ticket for the journey. Not put off by this detail, he duly boarded a train, changing at Crewe and Birmingham. Making the most of his situation, and perhaps working on the premise of 'In for a penny, in for a pound', he travelled in a First Class carriage. All went well until he was on the Crewe – Birmingham train and a guard conductor asked him for his ticket. He made a fuss of looking through his jacket and trouser pockets but was unable to produce one. Looking shocked, he told the guard conductor that he must have lost his wallet, which had contained a First Class ticket for Blackpool to Leicester and £170 in cash. He was advised that he should report the matter to the British Transport Police at Birmingham, where he would have to change to connect with the Leicester train.

Graham took this advice and walked into the BTP office at Birmingham New Street station, where he reported the loss of his wallet to the duty sergeant. He told the sergeant that he must have lost it on the train he was on, between Preston and Crewe. A statement was taken from Graham and details were phoned through to the BTP at Crewe so they could take action. With all the formalities completed, Graham continued his journey to Leicester.

Detectives at Crewe commenced enquiries and, looking into the matter carefully, found a number of inconsistences in Graham's statement. Although nothing conclusive had emerged, the officers' instincts were aroused and they contacted Birmingham for further information that would allow them to re-interview Graham. As a result, an investigation was initiated at Preston and eventually the file was sent to the BTP at Leicester for them to interview Graham again. They checked the information in the file and made some more enquiries. Having satisfied themselves with the facts, and with further evidence, they went to Graham's house and interviewed him closely. So closely in fact, that he admitted he had made up the story about the wallet, in order to avoid paying the train fare. He was then cautioned and informed that he would be prosecuted. His fabricated story had resulted in over twenty-six hours of police time being used, involving police officers in five different towns. The file was sent up to the director of prosecutions, who gave consent for Graham to be charged with wasting police time and fraudulent travel.

Graham appeared at Birmingham Magistrates' Court in March 1974, where he pleaded guilty to both charges. For the count of fraudulent travel, he was fined £10 and restitution of £4.70 for the fare, and for wasting police time he was fined £50 and ordered to pay £16.50 costs – a total of £81.20.

4

Vandalism and Railway Offences

Railways are a potentially dangerous environment for those who work and travel on them. They are also a source of fascination and interest for children and adults, who may be drawn to the railways for many reasons. There are a minority who take their curiosity further, and this can lead them to vandalise railway property in various ways, even putting passenger lives in danger by placing obstructions on the lines that could cause a derailment and have dire consequences. The law takes a serious view of these offences and the railway policeman has the task of enforcing the law, as well as investigating such crimes when they are committed. The following cases illustrate the fact that this crime has not just been a recent problem, but one that has been around since the early days of railway history.

The Case of the Runaway Trolley

The South Western Railway Company had built a new siding in the Kensington area of London to enable engines and carriages to be stabled, examined and repaired. It was not difficult for members of the public to gain access to the sidings, and young people especially were attracted to trespass here and get up to what they may have perceived as harmless mischief.

On the evening of 6 April 1887, William Sanders, an inspector of the South Western Railway who was stationed at Clapham Junction station, was walking through the sidings at Kensington. About 6.30 p.m. he saw a group of youths at the top of the sidings known as Sleeper Road. He went to the nearest signal box and instructed the signalman to inform the railway police. Forty-five minutes later, at 7.15 p.m. a carriage examiner named William Cotton was walking along the lines in the sidings when he spotted the same group of youths; as he watched, he saw one of them placing two pairs of trolley wheels on the track, then send them rolling towards the middle road and departure rails. Knowing that a London,

Chatham and Dover train was due, he ran after the wheels and, catching up with them, brought them to a halt and removed them from the rails before they could collide with the passenger train. He then went to the nearby South Western Railway Police office and reported the incident, giving a description of the youth.

The following evening, 7 April, Police Constable Jacob Lawrence was patrolling the sidings when he saw a group of youths walking between the rails. Aware of the previous evening's incident and the description of the youth who had placed the trolley wheels on the rails, he followed the group to the carriage examiner's hut, where he saw them pull the door down and go inside. He heard them causing mayhem and, as he neared the hut, he could see them knock the stove to pieces and kick the fire all over the hut. They then came outside and began throwing stones at the chimney pot until it was knocked down. Lawrence approached the youths who all ran off except one, leaving him to be arrested and taken to the nearest police box. While he was there, William Saunders came and identified the youth as one of the group he had seen earlier. When questioned, the youth gave his name as John Hall, aged seventeen years.

PC Lawrence took John Hall to the police office and presented him to Inspector Richard Edmonds. William Cotton attended the police office and identified Hall as the person he had seen place the wheels on the rails and send them off. Inspector Edmonds informed him that he would be charged with causing wilful damage to the carriage examiners' hut and with obstructing the railway line on the preceding night. Hall replied, 'What obstruction?' Inspector Edmonds answered, 'A pair of trolley wheels,' to which the reply came, 'I know nothing of the trolley wheels; I was there'. Hall was taken to the local Metropolitan Police station where he was booked into custody by PC 190, John Condon, of V division, and when Inspector Edmonds read the charges to him, Hall replied, 'It is a lie'.

On 25 April, John Hall appeared at the Old Bailey and was charged with only one offence – that of feloniously placing a pair of trolley wheels across the line of the London & South Western Railway Company, with intent to endanger the lives of passengers and obstruct engines and carriages using the railway. He pleaded not guilty, saying he knew nothing of the incident, but was found guilty and sentenced to eighteen months' imprisonment with hard labour, reflecting the seriousness of the crime.

Show me the Way to go Home

John Bull was an experienced engine driver on the London & South Western Railway, and used to dealing with all sorts of incidents that could befall an engine driver – this experience proved invaluable on 21 September 1896, when he was driving the 6 p.m. train from Portsmouth, due in to Woking at 7.51 p.m. The train was carrying more passengers than usual, as a great many had been attending the

Portsmouth town regatta day. The night was dark, it was raining and the train was drawing level with the bridge between Worplesdon and Woking when Bull felt the engine strike something, followed by the sound of a crash from underneath the train, which, fortunately, did not leave the rails. At this moment, the speed of the train, was about 45 miles an hour. As soon as he felt the crash, Bull shut off the steam but, finding that the train was running all right, he decided not to stop to avoid alarming the passengers.

He proceeded onto Woking station, slower than he would have done normally, and when he arrived at the station he alighted from his cab to examine the engine and found the brake gear had been badly damaged. He reported the matter to the station master, Uriah Sansom, who carried out his own examination of the damage. He then took another engine towards the bridge where the incident occurred and discovered a piece of iron rail embedded in the side of a sleeper that had been badly splintered. He took possession of the damaged rail and sleeper and returned to Woking station, where he informed the local police who, in turn, advised the railway police.

On 23 September, Detective Sergeant George Collins of the London & South Western Railway Police went to Woking police station and then, with Police Sergeant Marshall, proceeded to the village of Kemishford to interview William Clements, an eighteen-year-old youth who today might have been described as developmentally disabled. He had come to the notice of DS Collins after enquiries he had been making into the incident, but it was agreed that PS Marshall would lead the interview as he was known in the area and Clements might respond to him better than an officer who was a stranger to him. The officers found him at home and took him, along with his father, to Worplesdon railway station to conduct the interview. PS Marshall told Clements he was making enquiries into the obstruction placed on the railway lines two days previously and cautioned him.

Clements was asked about his movements on the night in question, to which he replied that he had left home about 8 p.m. and then walked along the road towards Worplesdon station, passing under the bridge and up the footpath to Mayford Bridge, by the side of the line. He walked from Mayford Bridge down to the post office and posted a letter that his mother had given him. He continued up the Guildford Road, past the Bird-in-Hand public house and Jackman's nursery, coming out by Woking police station, continuing underneath the railway bridge facing the new public hall. Clements changed his mind at this point and said that he took the road from Mayford to Woking, direct. The interview was concluded and the officers discussed what they had been told by the youth. They were not convinced by his account of his movements, as he had changed the story about the route he had taken and, even discounting that fact, there were inconsistencies. It was decided that a further, more official interview would be required to prompt Clements into telling the truth.

On 25 September, Clements was seen by PS Marshall who told him that the police were not satisfied with the differing accounts of his movements on the night of the 21st. He was arresting him and was to accompany him, along with his father, to Woking police station. Once there, Clements was questioned by Superintendent Robinson and then interviewed by DS Collins of the LSWR Police, with PS Marshall and Police Constable Fuller in attendance. Clements was asked again to explain where he had been and prompted that, this time, he should tell the truth. Clements was adamant that what he had told Superintendent Robinson was correct. He had left home and gone across Smart's Common to Mayford Bridge and down to the post office to post a letter for his sister. He returned to Mayford Bridge, where he went down onto the line, as he thought this would be the shortest and quickest way to Woking and meant he would not have to pass under Hook Bridge. While on the track, he tripped over something, which he thought was the metal line, hurting his knee and nearly ripping the toe cap off his boot. He showed the officers his boot to prove the point and apologised for going onto the track in the first place. It was clear that Clements was not telling the truth – his account of events was changing all the time. He was charged on two counts. Firstly, with feloniously placing a piece of iron rail on the railway with intent to endanger the safety of persons using the railway, and, secondly with the same offence, but with intent to injure persons using the railway.

William Clements appeared at the Central Criminal Court, on 19 October, where he pleaded not guilty to the charges. His explanation to the court was that he did not place anything on the railway line; he had gone down Smart's Common and along the road to Mayford to post a letter and never went near the track. When he got to the post office, he found he had missed the post and returned home at about 8.15 p.m. The next morning, he went to Woking station, got a stamp and posted the letter at the station, not at Mayford.

The jury, having heard all the evidence, retired to consider it fully. They returned a verdict of guilty and gave a recommendation for mercy to be shown in sentencing, as it was clear that the prisoner was of a weak intellect. The judge sentenced him to twelve months' hard labour.

Obstruction and Damage

Passengers travelling on the 7.25 p.m. train from Fenchurch Street to Shoeburyness, on 19 January 1957, were quietly reading, chatting or nodding off when the train suddenly came to a halt just outside Pitsea station. The driver jumped down from the engine and found a tree trunk wedged under the engine, damaging the automatic train control apparatus. The tree had been felled over a month before by railway maintenance staff, and the trunk placed near the line-side fence. An examination of the scene showed that the trunk had been dragged and placed across the rails, where it was struck by the train. No passengers or railway staff were injured, but considerable damage was caused to the train. The British Transport Commission Police were alerted to the incident and they, in turn, notified the local police.

Two weeks later, on 3 February, the 5.25 p.m. train from Shoeburyness to Fenchurch Street was travelling between Pitsea and Laindon when the driver felt a bump and saw an object knocked from the line. He stopped the train and found that the left-side engine-guard was missing. After reporting the incident, an examination of the scene found a large piece of timber, measuring 9 feet by 9 inches, lying by the side of the track, having obviously been struck by the train. There were 300 passengers on the train, which continued with its journey after a short delay. Railway maintenance men, walking along the line, later discovered that several signal glasses had been smashed between Basildon Hall and Basildon East, as well as all the window panes in a platelayer's cabin.

Earlier that morning, four young lads had been seen in Laindon High Street after a report of damage to property in the area had been received, and the local policeman passed this information to Pitsea police station. Following this incident, later that same afternoon, two Essex Constabulary officers were sent to investigate and, while walking over a railway bridge, they heard the sound of breaking glass and saw two signal lights go out. Hearing the sound of footsteps on the railway line, they shone their torches onto four young men, who proceeded to turn around and run. One officer gave chase and caught up with three of the men as they were crossing a nearby field. The other officer pursued the fourth man who had run in a different direction, but he managed to escape. The officers questioned the three men that were apprehended, who said they had been to the cinema and were taking a shortcut; the officers then took them to where the lights had been broken on the dovetail caution board, but on further questioning they denied any knowledge of the matter. However, a steel-framed catapult was found nearby and they were taken to Pitsea police station.

At the police station, the young men were identified as Smith, Bibby and Campbell and were told why they had been arrested and then questioned further about the incident that had taken place earlier in the evening. Smith admitted having a hand in the matter and made a statement owning up to damaging a petrol pump in Laindon and placing the timber across the railway line. He also admitted to having assisted in placing the tree trunk across the railway line, two weeks before, because he 'wanted to see the train break it up'. Once Smith had made his admissions, Bibby also confessed to his part in the incidents and said, in regards to the timber plank, 'We didn't try to hurt anyone, we only wanted to see the train push it off'. He also admitted his part in placing the tree trunk across the railway line with Smith, but said they didn't want to harm anyone, just see the engine push the tree off the track.

Later, in the early hours of the morning, a man called Reeves was stopped in the street by a police officer who knew that he tagged along with Smith, Bibby and

Campbell. He was told of their arrest and then was himself arrested on suspicion of placing the plank across the lines and damaging the signal lights. At the station, Reeves admitted his part in placing the timber but not breaking the signals. Campbell, who up to now had kept silent, spoke up and admitted smashing the signal lights and window panes.

The four were charged with the offences of (1) Placing wood across the railway likely to obstruct the railway; (2) Committing damage to a signal caution board; (3) Committing damage to the Basildon down signal and (4) Committing damage to Basildon Hall signal. Appearing at Chelmsford Assizes on 27 February, they all pleaded guilty. The judge gave a very severe summing up, accepting that they did not intend to injure passengers when they placed the tree trunk and timber across the lines but reminding them that they ought to have stopped and considered the possible consequences, which should have prevented the crime. This remark was in response to the charge of endangering life being dropped by the BTC Police. To damaging the signals, the judge said that the travelling public expected to be able to travel in safety, so he could not ignore the danger of this act of vandalism. Bibby and Smith were each sentenced to eighteen months' imprisonment for counts one and two, to run consecutively, and six months' for counts three and four to run concurrently – a total of two years' imprisonment. Reeves and Campbell each received eighteen months' imprisonment for count one, and six months' each on the remaining counts – a total of three years' imprisonment.

Going off the Rails

It was just another day for the British Transport Police sergeant and his three officers at Derby. On 5 March 1980, their working day started at 2 p.m., the late shift, and they went about their duties in the usual way, not expecting much to happen. It never did on the late shift; just the evening rush hour spent watching the commuters going home, seeing passengers alighting to catch connecting trains and then patrolling the station and surrounding area. However, on this particular day, that was all about to change and the officers were to be busier than they had anticipated.

At 6.30 p.m. the Derby – Crewe train left on time and the driver, Kenneth Austin, had no reason to suspect that his journey would be anything other than normal. The train travelled through the suburbs of Derby and, as it approached Peartree station, the driver felt the train strike something just before the station platform, causing the train to come off the rails. At 6.55 p.m. the telephone rang in the police office and was answered by the sergeant. The caller identified himself as the Derby Power Box controller and said, 'We have just had a report that the 18.30 hours, Derby – Crewe train has been derailed at Peartree station. The emergency services have been notified.'

The sergeant immediately instructed two officers to accompany him and left one behind in the police office to man communications and keep a log. The officers drove from Derby to Peartree station as fast as they could, and as the traffic would allow, to arrive at the scene. Peartree station was an unmanned station on the main Newcastle – Bristol line and this incident was sure to cause major rail disruption. The sergeant took charge of the scene and found a three-car diesel multiple unit underneath a road bridge that accessed the station. The train's front wheels were completely off the rails and the bogie frame was obstructing the opposite line. It was not long before the local police, fire brigade and ambulance service arrived on the scene and began their various duties to make the scene safe and to look after the passengers. There had been fifty-six passengers on board the train but, as luck would have it, none of them were injured. Their details having been taken, they continued their journey by road in coaches that had been laid on.

The BTP officers, assisted by the badly shaken train driver, made the lines safe to prevent any further accidents. When interviewed, the driver, Austin told them that the train had been travelling at 46 miles per hour and as he approached the station he had struck an object just before the platform, confirming the original information provided. Realising the seriousness of the situation, the sergeant made contact with the police office and asked that senior officers and the C.I.D. be informed of the incident, and he also requested their attendance at the scene. Before long, the divisional chief superintendent, chief inspector, inspector and a detective sergeant arrived, and with the local scenes of crime officer, their full investigation began to establish what had happened. It became apparent that the sleepers had been damaged and that the train had come to a halt 150 yards after hitting an obstruction and, in addition, there was damage to the station platform where the train collided with it. Items of debris were collected as evidence and, although the cause of the derailment was unknown at this stage, vandalism was strongly suspected.

The following day, the BTP were allowed to set up an incident room in Cotton Lane police station under the command of a detective chief inspector. The investigation became one of good old-fashioned police work, involving house-to-house enquiries, visiting local schools and making the usual appeals on radio and in newspapers. Such was the importance attached to this incident, the BTP were supported by both local CID officers and those from Nottinghamshire. The cause of the derailment had by now been established and it was found that a spare piece of rail had been placed across the line. The next day, the importance of the investigation was evident in the flurry of police activity in the local area, following up statements made the day before and making other enquiries.

A breakthrough happened the following day, 7 March, when an anonymous telephone call was received at the incident room giving the names of two schoolboys who were thought to have been involved. Two BTP detectives went to a local school and, in the presence of the headmaster, two boys, aged fifteen years, were interviewed and subsequently admitted to causing the derailment. They were arrested and charged with the offences of criminal damage, trespass on the railway and obstructing the railway and endangering the safety of passengers.

The boys duly appeared at Derby Juvenile Court and pleaded guilty to the charges. After pleas of mitigation were heard from their solicitor, they were both sentenced to three months in a detention centre. At the end of the case, the chair of the Magistrates congratulated the train driver on his prompt action, which had limited the effects of the derailment and ensured that the incident was not more serious. He also thanked the police for their speedy response on the night of the incident and for the investigation and hard police work that followed, finally bringing the offenders to justice. Good old-fashioned police legwork, door-to-door enquiries and public appeals had brought the case to a successful close.

Returning to the Scene of the Crime

On 1 October 1984, three youths made their way onto the railway track via a tunnel near Pembroke Dock and removed a number of rail clips that secured the sleepers to the line. They then cut a signal cable that ran from Pembroke Dock to Tenby. The youths threw some of the rail clips into a nearby pond and left the scene. The cable fault was detected and repaired by an engineer the following morning but, by the time he had returned to his depot, he was informed that the cable had been cut again in the same place. The youths had gone back to the same spot and, this time, removed sixty-four rail clips, throwing all of them into the pond, as before, and also severing the signal cable yet again. That afternoon, two of the youths went to the police station at Pembroke Dock and reported that they had seen a person with a punk hairstyle interfering with the rail line by the tunnel. The British Transport Police at Fishguard were alerted and they advised the rail controllers, who in turn cautioned the driver of a train due at Pembroke Dock to go across the rails with extreme caution.

On 4 October, the youths returned once more to the scene and, finding that the signal cable had been repaired, set about cutting it for a third time. They then contacted the local newspaper to tell them the story they had told the police. Officers of the BTP at Fishguard, who were investigating the original vandalism, decided to interview the two youths who had attended the Pembroke police station. The boys admitted their part in the vandalism and said that they had concocted the story about the person they had seen. They thought, by going to the local press, their story would be printed and would show them in a good light if they were found out and taken to court. The third boy was also questioned but denied any part in the act.

All three were charged with trespass on the railway, removing and stealing rail clips and causing damage to the signal cable. They appeared in the local juvenile court, where two of them pleaded guilty and the third, not guilty. The case was remanded to a later date, whereupon the third boy changed his plea. They were all admonished by the chair of the court, who said, 'You have pleaded guilty to various, serious charges and we feel that a custodial sentence is the only punishment appropriate.' The boys were sentenced to youth custody, two for three months and the third for twenty-eight days.

After the court hearing, the BTP issued a statement saying that if the Pembroke Dock Police had not been quick in reporting the incident, a very serious accident would have occurred and, in addition, the thorough investigation by their officers had brought the matter to a satisfactory conclusion.

5

Terrorism and Explosions

Railway stations have been a target for terrorist activity since the beginning of 1800. One reason for this is the effect of such an attack can be immense damage to property and a large number of casualties in a well-known public place, with the result that such an atrocity will attract maximum media coverage. The Fenian Dynamite campaign was a series of bombings that took place between 1881 and 1885 with the aim of bringing the Irish question to the heart of British politics, and the Metropolitan Railway Company's Underground system in London provided suitable locations for it to have just this result. The search for those who use violence with the aim of highlighting their political views has been a constant undertaking by the police forces in this country. This is no more so than for officers of the railway police, as the following cases illustrate.

The Charing Cross and Paddington Stations Explosions, 1883

There was nothing to indicate that the night of 30 October 1883 was to be any different from any other. Passengers travelling on the London Underground were going about their business as usual, perhaps noticing that it was busier than normal due to people returning home from a fisheries exhibition at Kensington. Around 8 p.m. two incidents of similar character occurred in two different places on the underground railway system, causing havoc and mayhem.

The platforms on the London Underground system at Charing Cross and Westminster Bridge stations, on the Metropolitan Railway District line, were scattered with passengers waiting patiently for their trains, chatting among themselves or reading the evening papers. Suddenly, an explosion occurred between the two stations, which were about half a mile apart, of sufficient force to blow plate glass out of buildings and plunge the platforms and stations into darkness; passengers at Charing Cross were thrown to the ground by the force of it. A train from Mansion House was just emerging from the tunnel onto the platform at Charing Cross when the explosion occurred, resulting in the lamps in carriages being extinguished and causing panic among the passengers. Rail staff were seen running from the station, leaving passengers to fend for themselves, and the huge clouds of black dust emerging from the tunnels only added to the panic and confusion. Any further train movement was stopped, which caused further chaos for the travelling public.

Officers of the Metropolitan Railway Company Police and the Metropolitan Police joined railway officials and engineers and walked the track between the two stations. Their purpose was to examine any damage and find a possible cause for the explosion. They soon ruled out this being gas, as lamps on the platforms were able to be relit not long after the incident. It transpired that the rails had not been damaged but the telegraph wires, which ran along the wall of the tunnel between the two stations, had been severely affected. Further examination of the scene resulted in the theory that the explosion could have been caused by a person or persons unknown igniting explosives before throwing them down one of the ventilators that took engine smoke from the tunnel to the surface. Without any evidence to back this up, the police were baffled and there the matter rested.

About the same time as the Charing Cross to Westminster Bridge explosion, a similar incident occurred near the Metropolitan Railway's Praed Street station, in Paddington. This time the consequences were more severe. The explosion happened close to a signal box, just outside the station, as a train was passing. The signal box was completely wrecked and six train carriages were damaged, injuring thirty-eight passengers, all of whom were taken to the nearby St Mary's Hospital, where many remained for further treatment. Such was the force of the explosion that houses in Praed Street, adjoining the station, and houses that backed onto the line had windows blown in.

A police investigation was started shortly after the incident. The team was headed by Superintendent Howard with Detective Inspector King and Detective Sergeant Cloake from the Metropolitan Police, and they were joined by Inspector Godson of the Metropolitan Railway Police. DI King and DS Cloake concentrated on gathering witness statements and other evidence. Superintendent Howard and Inspector Godson went to examine and analyse the scene of the explosion. The carriages had suffered extensive damage and the permanent way was littered with shards of glass and window sashes that had been blown out by the force of the explosion. The sleepers had been badly damaged, but the rails and the roof of the tunnel had not been damaged and further examination showed the path of the explosion to be along the wall and across the arch of the tunnel. A railway engineer discovered the site of the explosion. A gas pipe, one-and-a-quarter inches in diameter, was found in a twisted and upwards position; the engineer was of the opinion that the pipe could only have been affected in that way if an explosive force had been detonated below it and not as the result of a gas explosion. The possibility of a bomb being dropped from the window of the train as it passed the signal box was also considered unlikely, as it would have been difficult for anyone to enter the tunnel unseen, or without the risk of being struck by a passing train.

Following the investigation of both the Charing Cross and Praed Street station explosions, it was determined that they could not have been caused by any defects in gas pipes. It was the considered opinion that both explosions were committed by a group of unknown malicious people, intent on making some point or another, and seeking to instil fear into the public who used the Underground system to make their way around London. The government and the railway commissioners offered a substantial reward for information leading to the arrest and conviction of those responsible, but the response was poor and did not produce any more useful evidence. The case remains unsolved to this day.

The Charlton Street Signal Box Explosion of 1885

On 4 January 1885, the Metropolitan Railway, once again, suffered an explosion in one of its tunnels. This time, the target was another signal box at Charlton Street, located close to St Pancras Church in Euston Road, London, between King's Cross and Gower Street stations. The 8.53 p.m. Aldgate – Hammersmith train was stopped at the signal box and then allowed to proceed at 9.14 p.m. to Gower Street station (now Euston Square station) when the line was clear. The train had only gone 70 yards, when a loud report was heard, followed by an explosion. All the gas lights went out and the windows shattered in both the train and signal box. The train carried on to Gower Street station, where it stopped. Fortunately, there were not many passengers on board, but they were in state of shock and a few had been injured by broken glass from the windows. There was no damage to the woodwork or structure of the train and carriages; it was the signal box that had suffered the most, being shattered by the explosion, but fortunately no damage was caused to the signal levers and other equipment. The signalman described the floor of the signal box being heaved up and how, for a moment, he thought the box had been blown up.

The explosion was heard both at King's Cross and Gower Street stations, although only the platform at King's Cross was slightly damaged. Several houses above ground had their windows blown out and people rushed from their homes in fear of them collapsing.

Following reports of the explosion, officers from S Division of the Metropolitan Police were soon on the scene and set about calming the public. They ascertained that there were no serious injuries to be treated and, within half an hour, passengers were allowed to continue their journey from Gower Street station. An investigation was launched by the Metropolitan Police and Metropolitan Railway Police, led by Superintendent Harris and Chief Inspector Gosden respectively, who were soon on the scene. Gosden had experience of investigating such explosions as he was an inspector at the time of the Paddington station explosion, which occurred in 1883.

The train was examined and it was found that the rear Third Class carriage had been damaged the most, with windows having been blown out. The investigation moved to the tunnel, where it was discovered that a section of the brickwork, some 70 yards from the signal box, had been destroyed at a distance of 2 feet from the tracks. The roof showed evidence of the encrusted dirt and engine soot having been blown off, but no significant damage was suffered and it appeared that the rails and sleepers had escaped the effects of the blast. The telegraph cables, which run along the tunnel wall, were also undamaged. It was considered that the wall could be repaired.

The report from the Metropolitan Police and Metropolitan Railway Police concluded that a package containing explosives was left near the Charlton Street signal box, with intent to do damage to the railway and injury to people. There were no clues as to who committed the crime, which bore similar hallmarks to that of the Paddington station signal box explosion in 1883. Those responsible were never identified or caught.

The Aldersgate Station Explosion of 1897

On 26 April 1897, a Circle Line train, of the Metropolitan Railway Company, arrived at Aldersgate Street station (now renamed the Barbican) at 7 p.m. The train was crowded and so was the platform, as it was still the rush hour period. Within a few minutes, an explosion occurred, described at the time as 'like a small mine', causing panic and mayhem among the passengers on the platform and in the carriages of the train. The explosion, in a First Class carriage in the centre of the train, caused wreckage to be thrown into the air, injuring passengers and station staff. Gas lights on the platform were extinguished by the blast, plunging the area into semi-darkness and glass fell from the station roof, all adding to the confusion and panic. Passengers ran from the platform, crossing the rails on to the opposite side where the Chatham and Dover train had just departed, and any further trains were stopped from coming into the station. The explosion had completely destroyed the roof and sides of the carriage, making a large hole in the centre of the compartment that was about 3 yards in circumference; all that was left was the body of the carriage. Adjacent sections of the train were damaged and glass from the train was shattered and strewn across the area, along with splintered woodwork and other debris.

It was not long before the City of London Police, ambulances and medical help from the nearby St Bartholomew's Hospital arrived at the scene. There were ten casualties that required medical treatment, nine men and one woman. They were all taken to the hospital, where one of the male casualties, Henry Pitts from

Tottenham, who had been in an adjoining carriage and had sustained severe leg injuries and concussion, subsequently died soon after being admitted to hospital. Many other passengers suffered minor injuries and were treated at the station. The press were soon on the scene and secured interviews from several witnesses. One report was from the station master who said, 'I was standing just here by the bookstall on the central platform. Just as the train drew up I was sensible of a terrific explosion. My first impression was that something had come through the glass roof, for it was the splintering of glass which I first understood. Then all was confusion. Passengers came out from the carriages screaming, and demanding to know what had happened.' An initial examination of the scene and wrecked carriage took place and it concluded that there was the possibility a gas cylinder had exploded underneath the carriage, causing the tragedy.

The following day, an investigation by the railway company officials and Chief Inspector Palmer, with detectives of the City Police, was begun. There was concern that the explosion was caused to create a scare to coincide with forthcoming celebrations for Queen Victoria's diamond jubilee. The First Class carriage consisted of four compartments, all of which had been damaged to some extent or another. The only things remaining were two rear seats and the woodwork that separated the compartments. The explosion had occurred in the central section, underneath the seat near a window, on the platform side of the carriage. The damaged gas cylinder, initially thought to be the cause of the explosion, was carefully examined.

The original wall of Aldersgate station (now the Barbican station).

Illustration depicting the carriage exploding at Aldersgate station.

From inspecting the pressure gauge and records provided, it was shown that the cylinder was unlikely to have caused the explosion, as the amount of gas in it was below that which the cylinder was designed to hold; the angle of the steel frame of the carriage also pointed to it having been driven downwards by a force. This indicated that a powerful explosion had gone off, driving into the floor of the carriage and making a hole in the cylinder beneath. If the cylinder had been the cause of the explosion, then it, and the steel frame, would have been driven upwards. The conclusion was, taking into account all the other physical evidence, that the explosion had spent the maximum of its force in a downward direction rather than spreading longitudinally and upwards, and that the explosion was caused by a device planted under a seat in the central compartment of the carriage. A separate investigation undertaken by Detective Inspector Melville and his team, also of the City Police, made further enquiries and came out in favour of the above conclusion.

On the 30 April, an inquest into the death of Henry Pitts was opened and closed, pending further enquiries by the Board of Trade. On 24 May, the inquest was resumed at the City of London mortuary. Evidence was taken from station staff at Aldersgate station, who described the events of the day. The station inspector, by the name of Dowman, stated that he had felt the explosion, which was accompanied by a yellow-bluish light, and that the station filled with smoke and dust. On questioning, he said that he did not smell either gas or gunpowder. The guard of the train gave evidence that, as his train was pulling out of Farringdon Street station, a porter called out to him, saying he had seen smoke coming out from under one of the carriages. When the train arrived at Aldersgate, there was a loud report and the station was filled with smoke and dust. He, too, did not smell gas, but did smell a 'nasty, dry, hot smell'. The chief inspector of explosives, from the Home Office, gave evidence next. Colonel Majendie stated that he had examined the train's gas cylinder carefully and had no doubt that this was not the cause of the explosion. He and his team arrived at the conclusion that the explosion was caused by dynamite or gun-cotton, which had been put in a non-metal container and placed in the carriage at the Farringdon Street station, being designed to cause the maximum damage to railway property and also to harm people. The jury were asked to go out and consider the evidence and return with a verdict; when they did they had reached the conclusion that Henry Pitts was wilfully murdered by some person or persons unknown.

With the verdict from the coroners' court, the police opened a murder investigation but did not get any further with finding suspects and the case was closed as unsolved. Henry Pitts, who was a foreman with F. H. Ayres of 111 Aldersgate Street, left a widow and three children. A fund for Mrs. Pitts and her children was raised by the firm, its employees and some friends.

Gone in a Flash

Before the introduction of the system of paying wages directly into employees' bank accounts, it was the practice of British Transport Commission to pay workers weekly, in cash, at designated places within the area in which they worked. This responsibility was delegated to account clerks and an enormous burden of trust was placed on them. However, sometimes this trust was abused by those who gave way to temptation.

On the night of 19 July 1957, accounts clerk Coles and a colleague were assigned the task of paying out to the night duty staff at Stratford locomotive depot. Nothing untoward happened until just before 3 a.m., when the second clerk left the office. While he was away, the sound of an explosion came from inside the office. He returned quickly to see that a 'thunder flash' had exploded on a table, which was about 3 feet away from a window and on which were two boxes containing pay packets. There were flames on the table and Coles shut the lids of the boxes while his colleague poured water from a kettle on to the fire. The two men then ran outside but could not see anyone who may have thrown the 'thunder flash' through the open window. The incident was immediately reported to the British Transport Commission policeman on duty at Stratford, and the local Metropolitan Police.

Officers began an investigation that revealed that some of the pay packets had been slightly burned, but only a small amount of the paper money had been totally destroyed. The box was impounded so it could be examined by forensic experts later that morning. As the pay packets could not be issued, temporary arrangements were made for the workers to be paid as usual. Although no one had been hurt, Coles, who appeared to be suffering from shock, was allowed to visit the toilet and was later admitted to Queen Mary's Hospital at West Ham, where he remained until the Monday.

In the meantime, detectives worked on who could have caused the explosion and why. It was not until 22 July that it was discovered approximately £150 had been stolen from the pay boxes. It was now obvious why the explosion had been instigated but the question arose, who was the culprit? The obvious suspects were Coles and his colleague, so the police began looking into the background and financial circumstances of both men. Enquiries revealed that Coles was getting married on 27 July and had booked a honeymoon in Italy. He had borrowed from moneylenders and was behind on hire-purchase payments for furniture and household goods. In short, his financial position was precarious and suspect.

The day after he was discharged from hospital, he went to the travel agency, where he paid £51 for his honeymoon in Italy and exchanged £26 into foreign currency. He was carried away by his sudden access to money and he ordered and paid £6 for flowers to be sent to his fiancée and also purchased an expensive cigarette case and lighter for her. The police became aware of his spending and decided to bring him in for questioning.

On 25 July, Coles was interviewed by detectives and denied knowing anything more about the 'thunder flash' explosion than he had already told them. The detectives, who were certain they had the right man, pressed harder in their questioning; eventually, Coles broke down and admitted that it was he who had set off the 'thunder flash' while his colleague was out of the office, in order to cause a diversion as he stole wage packets from the pay boxes. He had secreted the packets in the yard when he asked to go to the toilet, shortly after the incident, and had gone back for them after leaving hospital.

Coles was arrested and charged with the theft of the cash and was lucky not have been charged with any explosives offences. He appeared at West Ham Magistrates' Court the following day, where he pleaded guilty and was sentenced to six months' imprisonment. Before sentence was handed down, the court was informed that Coles already had a criminal record for five offences of larceny and burglary and had served a term of Borstal training. Coles was further punished as he was not able to be married, the next day, to the girl he loved and never enjoyed the honeymoon they should have spent together.

Personal Belongings

The policeman is always looking around him, sorting out the normal from the abnormal, checking for that particular something that is either out of place or does not fit the surroundings. Very often, the seemingly small and trivial matter that arouses the curiosity of the officer can lead to something much bigger. This was the case one cold and wintry February night in 1958, when two British Transport Commission Police detectives were on observation duty at Liverpool's Lime Street station.

The detectives were following up a lead on goods being stolen from parcel vans during unloading, but the evening had not produced any results so far. It was about 10 p.m. when they decided to move off to somewhere warmer. Just as they were leaving, they saw a man walking across the station concourse, wearing a civilian overcoat over what appeared to be a uniform. Nothing out of the ordinary one may think, but what did catch their attention was the brand new suitcase that he was carrying. The man went into the station cafeteria and bought a cup of tea, then sat at a table facing the door. There was something not quite right about the man, so the detectives followed him into the cafeteria and sat down where they were in direct view of their suspect. There they sat for some time, employing an old police rouse nicknamed the 'fidget' technique, which involved letting the man see that they were interested in him and awaiting his reactions. It worked and the man got up, left his tea, and exited the cafeteria, swiftly followed by the detectives. Once outside, the suspect was stopped by the two officers and questioned about the suitcase that he was carrying. The man told them where he had bought it, how much it cost and stated that it only contained his personal belongings.

Concerned by these answers and the general demeanour of the man, they took him to the police office in the station, where they asked him to open the suitcase. The suitcase was locked and the man said he had lost the keys. The problem was soon overcome; the case was opened and the personal belongings turned out to be 500 rounds of .45 revolver ammunition, in packets wrapped up in newspaper. The detectives, not unnaturally surprised by the contents of the suitcase, then searched the man and emptied his pockets. They found a sealed envelope and, when this was opened, another sealed envelope was discovered inside, which contained two pieces of paper. One piece had a letter and number code written on it, while the other had an address in Dublin. Enquires were made into the identity of the man with the suitcase who was, unsurprisingly, not very co-operative. It was established that the man was Shamus McCallum, an Irishman, who was employed by the Liverpool Corporation Omnibus Company as a conductor.

The detectives then arrested McCallum and transported him to the Liverpool City Central police station, where he attracted the attention of officers of the Special Branch, who interviewed him closely. After a lengthy interview and questioning, McCallum finally admitted he was a member of the Irish Republican

Army but would not say any more. He was eventually charged with four offences under the Firearms Act and Explosive Substances Act.

Shamus McCallum appeared at the Liverpool Spring Assizes and, when asked to plead, he said, 'As a member of the Republican Army, I am not in a position to recognise the authority of this court.' The judge, Mr Justice Oliver, directed that the jury should be sworn in to consider whether McCallum was mute of malice or by visitation of God. The jury immediately decided the former and, as a plea of not guilty was entered, the case proceeded. McCallum was found guilty and sentenced to six years' imprisonment, closing an interesting case that had been initiated by the observations of two sharp-eyed railway police officers.

Lady Luck and the Bomb Hoax

On 13 September 1973, Jack Mellor, the station master of Bournemouth station, was working in his office, completing some last-minute paperwork before he could think of going home. At 4.50 p.m. there was a knock at his door and a seventy-year-old man came into his office and handed him an envelope. Opening the envelope immediately, the station master pulled out a white card with a message, made out of letters cut from a newspaper, which read, 'Bombs on the track between Boscombe and Bournemouth'. The station master looked up from the card, only to see that the man had left before there was time to question him. He immediately contacted the British Transport Police office on the station, where the only officer on duty was a probationary constable who had been in the force for just a few months. He and the station master made arrangements for a search of the line to take place between Bournemouth and Pokesdown, looking for any packages or suspicious objects. Trains were temporarily suspended from travelling on that section of the line, causing major disruption of services.

The constable had obtained a description of the man who handed in the envelope from the station master, and began to search the surrounding area. Looking in the British Railways Staff Club, next to the station, he found his man and took him back to the police office on the station. The officer began questioning him and he gave his name as Joseph James Beckinsale. He told the officer that he had been in the railway staff club at lunchtime, when he was approached by a man, who he knew slightly, and asked if he would like to earn a couple of pounds. Beckinsale readily agreed, and was handed an envelope with the instructions to give it to the station master at 4.45 p.m. that evening. On further questioning, he said that he didn't know the man well, or where he lived or worked, but thought his name was Brian. By this time, the constable was joined by a colleague and, after changing into civilian clothes, together they made enquiries from staff working on the station, the immediate area and the staff club. No one could positively identify 'Brian' but they managed to get a rough description and, as the envelope had been given to

84

Beckinsale in the club, they decided to keep a watch on the premises. A couple of hours later, a man answering their description walked into the club, swiftly followed by the two officers, who then identified themselves and explained what they were enquiring about. The man denied knowing anything about the hoax and added that he was working at the time. The officers then told him that they were looking for a man called Brian and that he answered the description they had been given. At this point, he was arrested and cautioned, to which he responded that he only did it for a joke.

The man was taken to Bournemouth police station and questioned further. He told the officers that his full name was Brian Thomas Joseph Johnson and he worked as a cook for British Railways Catering Services on the Bournemouth to London trains. He said that his reason for making the hoax bomb threat was that he wanted to finish work early and thought that, by delivering the message when he did, the 6.34 p.m. train from Southampton to Waterloo that he was to work on would be cancelled. His house was searched and officers recovered two newspapers that had been cut up. The letters missing from the newspapers matched those on the piece of card that made up the hoax message. He was charged without lawful excuse, that in a letter to one Jack Mellor, being the manager of Bournemouth railway station, he had made a threat, intending that the said Jack Mellor would fear it would be carried out, to destroy or damage the railway line between Boscombe and Bournemouth, belonging to the British Railways Board.

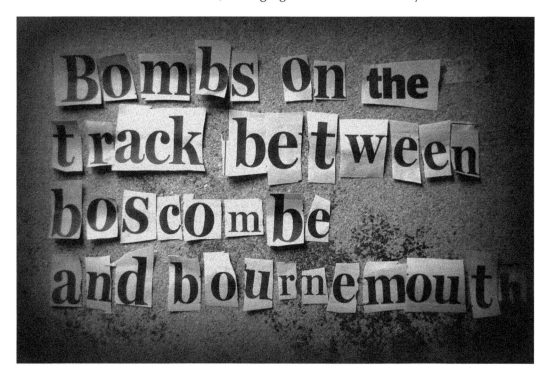

Impression of what the Boscombe and Bornemouth bomb hoax message may have looked like.

Brian Johnson appeared at Bournemouth Magistrates' Court on 9 October, where he pleaded guilty to the charge; he was sentenced to three months' imprisonment and ordered to pay the prosecutions costs. Joseph Beckinsale was considered to be an innocent person in the incident and no charges were brought against him.

The probationary police officer, who had only a short period of service, was praised for the initiative he had shown in making enquiries to locate Beckinsale and for his part in successfully finding him, despite the station and surrounding area being crowded with hundreds of people. Good police work and lady luck certainly played their part that evening.

The West Ham Tube Train Bombing, 1976

On 15 March 1976, the 4.39 p.m. Hammersmith – Barking, Metropolitan Line (now the Hammersmith & City Line) train, driven by motorman Julius Stephen, left on time to start its journey from Barking through the crowded stations of Liverpool Street, King's Cross, Baker Street, Paddington and others, towards its termination at Hammersmith. The train made its scheduled stop at West Ham station and then, after passengers had alighted and boarded the train, it went on its way. The train

The westbound platform at West Ham Underground station.

was less than a mile from the station when at 4.45 p.m. an explosion occurred in the leading carriage of the train, injuring several passengers. Following the explosion, the train stopped and a man was seen to jump down from the carriage and onto the track. At almost the same time, Julius Stephen alighted from the driver's cab onto the track and walked towards the front of his train, waving his arms to attract the attention of an oncoming train in order for it to stop. As he was waving, he came face to face with a man and a scuffle took place; the man raised a gun and shot Julius Stephen who fell, mortally wounded.

Standing on the platform was Peter Chalk, a Post Office engineer. He heard the explosion and immediately thought it was a bomb that had gone off; his worst fears were confirmed as he saw debris from the leading carriage spew over a wide area of the track and beyond. He ran along the platform and onto the track, his first thought being to help any casualties. He found some injured passengers there and told them he was going to get help. He then boarded the carriage to see if anyone was trapped in the wreckage. As he did so, he came face to face with the gunman, his clothes torn and covered in blood, who was reloading his gun. Peter Chalk told the gunman he only wanted to help the injured and moved forward to pass him; he was 4 feet beyond the gunman when he was shot in the chest and fell among those he was trying to help.

A police constable from the Metropolitan Police, travelling in his panda car, heard the explosion and immediately drove to a road running parallel to the railway track. As he got out of his car, he saw the gunman, who had alighted from the carriage and was standing at the front of the train. The gunman warned the constable that he was armed and fired a shot that fortunately missed him, before running off towards West Ham station. The constable got on his personal radio and gave an account of what had happened, while getting into his panda car and reversing up the road some 50 yards. He got out of the car and saw the gunman walking towards him along the railway track; on seeing the constable, the gunman took deliberate aim and fired at him, missing once more. During this second attempt on his life, the officer continued to give a running commentary on his radio.

The gunman made his way to the station and threatened several people as he continued along the platform and down the exit, onto the street. Meanwhile, Police Constable Raymond Kiff, who had been listening to his colleague's commentary, had gone to the station and then made his way onto the platform before jumping down onto the track to look for the gunman. While he was on the track, he heard shots coming from the booking hall and so he climbed back onto the platform and ran down the stairs, towards the sound, and then onto the street. There, on the pavement, he saw the gunman lying with the revolver held in both his hands. PC Kiff went to tackle him but he got up and ran off along the street, brandishing the gun and turning and threatening him with it as he went. PC Kiff decided to follow him on the opposite side of the street.

The gunman went into a factory yard and PC Kiff, still close behind, took cover behind a van that was parked opposite the factory entrance. He looked through the van window, into the yard, and saw the gunman lying in a semi-prone position, appearing to be taking aim at something or somebody. PC Kiff drew his truncheon and ran across the road, towards the factory, where he jumped onto the gunman's back, striking him with his truncheon and immediately disarming him. He turned the gunman over to affect an arrest and saw that the gunman had shot himself in the chest.

After the incident, the anti-terrorist squad from Metropolitan Police were assisted by British Transport Police officers from Force Headquarters and the London Transport Area in their investigation into what had happened. The forensic evidence gathered from the scene had all the hallmarks of previous bombs that had been made by the Provisional Irish Republican Army. The gunman was identified as Adrian Vincent Donnelly, aged thirty-seven years, a steel fitter and member of the IRA living in London. Witnesses in the front carriage said they saw Donnelly throw a holdall with smoke coming out of it from one end of the carriage to the other, shortly before it exploded. The bomb was estimated to have contained 5 lbs of explosives and was meant to have been detonated at a station during rush hour to cause the maximum loss of life and damage. However, it was evident that the bomb had been triggered prematurely, resulting in Donnelly throwing the holdall containing the bomb away so he would not be injured. Eight people were hurt in the explosion on board the carriage. One man suffered a fractured leg when a carriage door struck him after it was blown over 100 yards.

Donnelly stood trial for murder, attempted murder and causing an explosion with intent to kill or endanger life, along with two other men; they all refused to enter a plea, so a not guilty plea was entered by the court. The trial took place at the Old Bailey and lasted thirty-one days. The jury deliberated for five days and returned with a verdict of guilty to all the charges against the three men. Mr Justice Croom-Johnson, the presiding judge, before passing sentence, told Donnelly, 'You seem to regard human life to be taken as easily as other people would light a cigarette ... You are a very dangerous man and it is right that you should be removed from public life and contact with other human beings for as long as possible.'

Donnelly was sentenced to five life sentences with a recommendation that he serve thirty years for the murder of Julius Stephen, the attempted murder of Peter Chalk and for causing the explosion on the tube train on the same day. He was further jailed for life for the attempted murder of two police officers, who he had shot at that day. He was handed a twenty-year sentence, to run concurrently, for having explosives at his home in South Brixton.

The bravery of three men, on that fateful day, did not go unrecognised. PC Kiff was awarded the George Medal for gallantry and devotion to duty of a very high order, in facing Donnelly, a dangerous and armed terrorist, knowing that he had already caused a bomb explosion and mortally wounded a man. The Queen's Gallantry Medal was awarded, for gallantry and complete disregard for their safety when faced with the armed terrorist, to Julius Stephen (posthumously) and Peter Chalk.

6

Cases of Special Interest

There are some crimes that do not happen often and, consequently, when they do they become of special interest, not only to the police but the public as well. During the course of investigating such cases, other crimes are sometimes brought to light and are dealt with alongside the original offence. These crimes would not normally be seen on the railways and would be thought of as most unlikely to occur there. The following cases show that this assumption can sometimes be wrong, as well as illustrating the versatility of the railway policeman.

The Case of the Indian Takeaway

Railway stations attract many people with criminal intent who employ various methods to capitalise on the particular situations that occur in this environment. One such example is the con man who concentrates on passengers that have just arrived and are obviously visitors, new to the area.

In the early months of 1959, a con man, an Indian, preyed on his own countrymen when they arrived at Victoria station in London on the weekend 5.25 p.m. Dover – London service. Many well-to-do Indians who were travelling from India to England used to disembark from the P&O liners at Marseilles and take the overland train, calling at Lyons, Paris, Calais and London (Victoria). By taking this journey, they could arrive in England two or three days earlier than if they remained on board their ship.

Our con man generally used the same *modus operandi* each time to trick his fellow countryman into parting with money. Speaking in his native tongue, he would approach his intended victim and tell him that he had been in England a long time and knew the best hotels for Indians, adding that there were a lot of wicked people in London who would take advantage of any newcomers; it was fortunate that he had met him so that he could can steer him clear of the many pitfalls that he may encounter. Having gained the confidence of his victim, our con man would spin a yarn and deprive him of cash, then disappear, leaving him bewildered and penniless. It was not long before complaints were being received by the British Transport Commission Police at Victoria station regarding the approaches made by the con man and the various ploys he used to obtain money, but it was difficult to get a good description of him from his victims due to the language barrier.

Complaints continued to come in about the con man from Indians who had been fleeced, but, despite enquiries and observations by CID officers, there was little progress; what was needed was a breakthrough and, fortunately, it eventually came about. An Indian doctor, who had been resident in England for many years, made a complaint that one of his students, Mr Patel, on arrival at Victoria station had been approached by an Indian who had taken him to a hotel, where he 'robbed' him of all his English money. The *modus operandi* in this case was that, on being taken to the Brighton Hall Hotel in Russell Square, the student was told that it was always the custom in England to have a bath immediately on arrival; he fell for this and undressed, then went to wash. While the student was bathing, the con man went through his clothing and wallet and stole the loose cash, which amounted to £5, before leaving the hotel.

The doctor, aware of the ongoing problem, was most indignant and demanded that if something was not done about the matter, he would formally complain to the Indian Embassy. Having been assured that his complaint, along with those already made by other victims, would be, and had been, receiving close attention, the doctor was able to describe the con man as a young Indian male, smartly dressed, with a small lump or wart on his left cheek and having the appearance of a university student.

The following weekend, a C.I.D. officer was detailed to keep observations on the platform where the 5.25 p.m. Calais–Dover boat train would arrive. While he was watching, he noticed a smartly dressed Indian man waiting on the platform, reading a paper; his suspicion was further aroused when he noticed a lump on the Indian's left cheek. He realised he had found the con man. He kept his suspect under close observation and did not have to wait long before he could witness him in action. When the train arrived, two Indian gentlemen, wearing their native clothing, alighted from the train and passed through the ticket barrier; the con man had noticed them and made his approach. After the usual introductions of raising his hat and bowing, he attempted to engage the men in conversation using his native tongue of Hindustani. Unfortunately for him, it became clear that the two passengers were not willing to accept his help as they looked blankly at each other and nodded their heads uncertainly, as if to say 'Who on earth is this man?' The detective, having spotted the passengers' reaction, moved closer to hear and see more of what was happening. At this point, however, the con man turned and noticed him watching nearby and, probably becoming suspicious, ended the conversation mid-sentence, raised his hat and began to leave the station, closely followed by the detective. The con man, realising he had been rumbled, began to walk faster, almost breaking into a run, but was stopped by the detective, who told him he answered the description of an Indian who had met a fellow countryman at Victoria station the previous Friday and later stolen the man's cash at a hotel. The con man denied this, stating that the man was his friend and he had travelled on the boat train with him.

Knowing he had his man, the detective cautioned and arrested the suspect and took him to the police office on the station for further questioning. During the interview, the con man, much to the delight of the detective, incriminated himself by saying, 'I have done nothing wrong. Is my friend going to charge me? I only borrowed the money.' The 'friend', Mr Patel, was contacted and identified him as the man who had approached him at Victoria station and led him to the Brighton Hall Hotel. The con man was charged with the theft of £5 from Mr Patel and appeared, the next day, at Clerkenwell Magistrates' Court. When asked how he was pleading, the con man replied in broken English, 'I am a stranger here; I don't know what it means.' A plea of not guilty was entered. Evidence of the arrest was given and the detective asked for a remand in custody, whereupon, the prisoner immediately asked for bail; the magistrate looked up over his glasses and replied, 'You say you are a stranger and you have the audacity to ask me for bail. I think it would be better if we looked after you for a week.'

During the remand period, the police made further enquiries and found that the con man had a criminal record in this country, having been convicted of a similar crime twelve months before. Contact was made with a previous complainant, Mr Goyal, who had also been met at Victoria by the accused and had been spun a story and taken round to Thomas Cook's offices in Ludgate Circus. Here, he was persuaded to cash a traveller's cheque for £20 and the con man took this money, saying he would look after it as there were a lot of rogues around and he would now take Mr Goyal to a tailor's shop so he could purchase some western clothes to replace his native garments. Taking him to a 'fifty-shilling tailors' in the Strand, he paid the deposit on a made-to-measure suit from the £20 he had taken possession of, and arranged to meet Mr Goyal at Hyde Park Corner. It should come as no surprise that he did not turn up to meet Mr Goyal at the appointed place and time.

At the remand hearing, a further charge of stealing £17 from Mr Goyal was added and when asked how he was to plead to the two charges, the con man pleaded guilty. The magistrate remanded him for a further week and asked the police to find out the movements of the prisoner for the past three years. Enquiries were made at the Indian Embassy, who stated that the con man was known to them and they had received complaints about his activities, but they did not wish this information to be made public, having regard to the political situation in India at the time and for diplomatic reasons. The police in Paris came forward with information that he was known to them also, as a confidence trickster. It also transpired that he had come to England in 1952 as a railway student, but had failed his exams and complaints about him began four years later.

At the remand hearing, the magistrate was given this information in a closed court so as to comply with the Indian Embassy's request. Asked if he had anything to say before being sentenced, the con man replied, 'I do not want to stay here, I would like to go back to my own country and my own people.' The magistrate, Mr Pope, sentenced him to six months on the first charge and six months on the second charge to run consecutively, a total of twelve months' imprisonment, and added caustically, 'I think that will be long enough for you to get in touch with your people in India, and for them to make any arrangements to get you back there.'

Not Spending a Penny, but Collecting Them

Millicent Manning had been working for British Railways for eighteen years as an attendant in the ladies' room at Darlington Top Bank station (now Darlington railway station). She was fifty-eight years old, of slight build, weighing all of 6 stone, and married; her husband also worked for British Railways and they lived in a good residential area of Darlington. Her colleagues on the station thought of her as rather odd or eccentric and there was a common belief that she fed her husband on scraps of food and that she, despite her build, was the dominant force in the family.

Millicent had come to the attention of the British Transport Commission Police at Darlington, being suspected of taking pennies from women who wished to make use of the toilets at the station and then pocketing the money that should, of course, have been put into the toilet automatic locks. Her method was to open the toilets for the women with her pass key, on the pretext of looking in to make sure they were clean, and then to ask for the pennies, which she kept for herself. The investigation was passed to Policewoman (CID) Armin, stationed at Darlington, who enlisted the help of Policewoman Sergeant McDonnell and policewomen Crawley and Robertson, from the plain-clothes section of Newcastle Division. Various items and money, which had been marked for identification purposes, were placed inside a handbag and a plan was devised to see if Millicent would take the bait.

Policewoman Robertson visited the ladies' room and handed the test handbag to Millicent, on pretext that she had found it in the toilet she had just used, and observations were then kept on Millicent's movements. She was seen to take the handbag to the station's lost property office and hand it in. Policewoman Crawley then collected the handbag and, on examining it, found that a one-shilling coin had been removed from the various coins that were left inside it. Following the discovery, Millicent was interviewed by the officers and she said she had lots of shilling coins with scratch marks on them and that she had not taken any money from the handbag, handing it to the lost-property office intact. When questioned further, Millicent did admit that she had taken a shilling from the lost handbag before handing it in. Her locker was searched and the officers found four dog biscuit bags that contained coins adding up to nineteen shillings in silver coins and ten pence in copper coins. She was arrested and told that she would be charged with the theft of the shilling coin from the handbag. But the investigation did not stop there.

Millicent agreed to accompany the officers to her home, which was found to be in an appalling condition. An upstairs room was searched and property belonging to the British Transport Commission and hotel and catering services was discovered, with a value of £11 19s 4d. When asked to open the other two rooms, Millicent refused, saying that she had lost the keys. The officers left and, the following day, obtained a search warrant from the magistrates' court in Darlington. They returned to Millicent's house with the warrant but she again refused to unlock the doors, resulting in the officers having to force their way in. The doors would only open a few inches and it took some effort to squeeze through into the rooms. Once inside, the officers were astonished at what they saw.

Each room was stacked with items of nearly every description: clothing, dozens of pairs of shoes, ladies' handbags, suitcases, parcels of unopened shopping, packets of foodstuffs including bacon, butter, cheese and meats, still wrapped as by the shop on the day they were purchased, and numerous packages of coal and firewood. In the centre of each room there was a bed, piled high with the items and, once these had been removed, on the mattresses were found fifty-nine dog-biscuit bags filled to the brim with copper coins. When counted, it was discovered that the money amounted to £55 5s 4d. As if to confirm the stories of her odd and eccentric behaviour, the officers found a joint of beef under one of the mattresses that had been there some considerable time. Millicent's husband, when interviewed, recalled that he had only had a few mouthfuls of the joint before it had been taken away from him, never to be seen again. A dressing table revealed unopened wage packets totalling £1,060 12s 12d. Millicent explained that she did not like to pay tax on money deposited in the bank and stated that she had about £10,000 tucked away. The condition of the house, which was considered a health risk, was brought to the attention of the local medical officer of health, who ensured steps were taken to clean the house up and make it safe and habitable.

Millicent made a statement, admitting to stealing money totalling between two and three shillings each day over a period of seven years that should have been put into the toilet automatic locks. In agreement with her solicitor, it was decided that Millicent should pay restitution of £100, in addition to the sum of £55 6s 4d, which is the amount she was charged with stealing. No charges were preferred regarding the stolen items that were found.

Millicent's mental health was considered bizarre and she was sent to a local institution for treatment prior to the court hearing. She appeared before Darlington

Magistrates' Court and pleaded guilty to four counts of larceny. The court heard the full facts of the case and her solicitor pleaded mitigating circumstances due to her mental state. She was placed on probation for two years, one of which should be spent in the institution where she would continue her treatment. The case had caught the attention of the daily newspapers who reported all the facts, with the headline 'Millicent the Magpie' appearing in one of them and summing up the situation aptly. For the police, the case was successful on two counts; firstly, Millicent had been caught and convicted of the long-term theft of money, and secondly, Millicent's mental health issues had been highlighted and this ensured she received treatment for her illness, showing the often unsung social care side to police work.

The Other Side of the Coin

It was an offer that could not be refused. How often has this saying been heard quoted, when the opportunity to purchase something of value and at a fraction of the true cost presents itself? For three Harwich boat train, dining-car attendants, this was exactly the situation they found themselves in. During the course of 1969, a Mr Plooij, an antiques dealer of Dutch nationality, became a regular passenger on the Harwich boat train and, consequently, was known by the dining-car staff. As is often the case, this familiarity led to Mr Plooij becoming more intimate with the staff and he took advantage of this with an offer he made them, one they found impossible to refuse.

Mr Plooij gave his new-found friends the chance to purchase what appeared to be genuine gold sovereigns, half sovereigns and American twenty-dollar pieces at a price that was well below the market value. So great was the temptation to make a possible financial gain, the dining-car staff purchased more of the coins when they were offered on two further occasions. It was not long before the staff decided to sell their coins and realise the profit they anticipated making. However, it was not to be, as they soon discovered that the coins they had purchased were in fact counterfeit and completely worthless. Irked by having been duped and also the fact that they lost a considerable amount of money, the dining-car attendants reported the matter to the British Transport Police at Harwich.

CID officers at Harwich took the attendants' statements and commenced enquiries and, due of the serious nature of the crime and the involvement of a foreign national, also made contact with Metropolitan Police Special Branch, who were fully apprised of the crime and the suspect. Through this liaison, Special Branch requested that they be present when Mr Plooij next came through Harwich, so he could be stopped and identified by the complainants. The police at Harwich agreed to facilitate this and awaited the next visit by the suspect.

On 28 June 1969, Mr Plooij, accompanied by his wife, arrived at Harwich and, as he was driving his van off the boat, was stopped by customs officers on the request of Special Branch. The couple and their van were thoroughly searched and a cigarette packet in Mrs Plooij's handbag was found to contain twenty-four gold sovereigns. The BTP investigating officers were informed and were present when Mr Plooij was brought to Harwich railway station, where he was identified by the dining car attendants as the man who had sold them coins on three separate occasions. Both Mr and Mrs Plooij were arrested and charged with going equipped to cheat under the Theft Act 1968 and brought before a special court, where they were remanded in custody. Subsequent court appearances were made as the case was investigated further, and both were later given bail upon the surrender of their passports.

The coins were sent to the Royal Mint and were examined by a chemist and assayer. They came to the conclusion that the coins were in an excellent condition, but were definitely counterfeit. The American twenty-dollar piece was dated 1903, the sovereigns dated 1917 and the half-sovereigns 1902 and 1913. It was discovered that there was a slight variation in size and weight from genuine coins. The counterfeit coins contained an amount of gold and were valued at £80; they would have fetched £310 if they were genuine coins. The Plooijs could have made a sizable profit from these recovered coins, as they presumably had from the ones they sold the unfortunate dining-car staff.

The investigation became complex, with evidence of various offences being put forward, and the case was sent to the Director of Public Prosecutions for consideration of charges under the Coinage Offences Act 1936. The DPP instructed that the Plooijs both be charged with possession of twenty-four counterfeit coins for sale, and that Mr Plooij meet additional charges of uttering counterfeit coins on three separate occasions.

Both appeared before a summary trial, the defendants agreeing to this course of action and pleading guilty to the charges. Mitigating circumstances were offered by the defence to the effect that the couple had already been held in custody and, even though they had been given bail, they had been unable to see their children. Mrs Plooij was given a conditional discharge. Her husband was fined £10 on each of the uttering offences. He was also ordered to pay the prosecution's costs of £10 and the £10 10s fee for the interpreter, who had been present at police interviews during their charging with the offences and the subsequent court appearances. What happened to the counterfeit coins? They were returned to the Royal Mint, as the law demands.

The Helping Hand

Stanley Passmore was a twenty-nine-year-old, fanatical trainspotter who lived in Bristol. There was not much that he didn't know about trains, stations or how the railways were organised and operated. His interest almost bordered on obsession, so much so that he was able to use this knowledge to his own advantage and for financial gain.

On 13 September 1971, there was a derailment of coal wagons at Flax Bourton, Bristol, resulting in coal being strewn over a wide area. The Up and Down main line, between Bristol and Weston-super-Mare, was blocked and train services were disrupted for several days. An emergency bus service was put in place between the two stations, calling at stations en route, the contract for which was awarded to a local coach firm run by a Mr Turner. On the first day of the derailment, the coach firm was approached by a man who presented himself as being an employee of British Railways and, saying he was authorised by the Bristol area manager, Mr Hall, organised the coach services being supplied. The man, who was of course Stanley Passmore, applied himself to organising the replacement buses, and his aptitude and knowledge in respect to the train services from Bristol impressed Mr Turner.

Passmore was seen frequently at Bristol, Yatton and Weston-super-Mare stations, organising the vehicles, directing passengers onto the correct coaches for their destinations and giving instructions to the drivers as to where they were to go; he was also seen late at night, at stations along the route, ensuring the smooth running of this emergency service. During the three days that the line was blocked, Passmore was not questioned about his authority by railway staff or the drivers of Turners Coaches. The staff at Bristol, Yatton and Weston-super-Mare were so impressed by the authoritative and efficient manner in which Passmore dealt with the situation at each station that they were of the opinion that the service provided would not have run as smoothly if he had not been present. An example of Passmore's effectiveness was shown at Yatton station, where passengers were awaiting transportation to Bristol station. They had been kept waiting for some time even though coaches were standing at the station. Passmore turned up and instructed passengers to board the coaches and then, after finding the drivers at a local hostelry, partaking of refreshments, ordered them back to the station to take the coaches and passengers on to Bristol.

Passmore's enthusiasm knew no bounds. Two days after the derailment, on 15 September, Passmore turned up at Bristol Temple Meads station and found that eight workers for the Ford Motor Company had been waiting thirty minutes for their train. Passmore, not liking the fact that the workers had been kept waiting that long, telephoned Turners Coaches and ordered a fifty-three seater luxury coach, which duly arrived at the station and took the workers to Severn Tunnel Junction. Following this, Passmore decided that he would go to Flax Bourton and ordered a chauffeur-driven car to take him. Once there, he introduced himself as Mr Hall, the Bristol area manager, and carried off his deception so well that he received all the respect that this position would merit. Passmore decided that his hard work for British Railways warranted remuneration and set about offering coal from the derailed wagons to BR staff, at twenty-five pence a hundredweight. Coal at this knocked-down price soon resulted in favourable sales, with the purchasers being informed that the proceeds would be donated to the Railway Orphanage. Passmore gave his customers receipts for the coal and signed them in the name of Mr Hall.

Following the hire of the luxury coach to Severn Tunnel Junction on 15 September, the owner of the coach firm, Mr Turner, became suspicious and contacted the real Mr Hall, assistant passenger manager at Bristol. Hence, he discovered that Passmore had no authority to order the coach and, in fact, was not employed by British Railways in any capacity. The matter was reported to the British Transport Police at Bristol, who began an investigation. As enquiries progressed, detectives found suspicion centring on Stanley Passmore, who was known to many for his trainspotting activities, and was identified by staff from a photograph. Having found sufficient evidence and with a positive identification, investigating officers went to Passmore's home and arrested him. He was interviewed and questioned about the hiring of the coach and chauffeur-driven car on 15 September; he admitted committing the offences and was subsequently charged under the Theft Act 1968. Following information received and further enquiries, Passmore was questioned about the bargain coal sales and he admitted to these offences also and was charged accordingly.

On 29 September, Passmore appeared at Bristol Magistrates' Court. However, five minutes before the hearing, the BTP investigating officer was approached by detectives from Bristol City Police, who suspected Passmore of being responsible for offences committed in Cardiff, although details had not been circulated, nor

Bristol Temple Meads station.

had a warrant for his arrest been issued. Passmore pleaded guilty to the offences committed on the railway and was fined a total of £80. Following his hearing, he was arrested by BCP to await an escort from the South Wales Constabulary.

During subsequent interviews with the SWC, it transpired that Passmore had approached young trainspotters at Cardiff General railway station, saying he was organising a coach trip to Scotland for trainspotters. Many of these fellow enthusiasts sent money to Passmore at his home address to pay for seats, but the coach never arrived to pick them up. Further enquiries revealed that he had also approached passengers and trainspotters at Derby railway station with a similar offer and they had also sent money to his home address; of course, as before, the coach never turned up for the trip. The BTP agreed for the SWC to deal with these offences, in addition to their own charges, and Passmore was bailed to appear at Cardiff Magistrates' Court at a later date.

While on bail, BCP received complaints that Passmore had obtained the name and address of the wives of three men who had been sentenced to imprisonment for robbery at Bristol Assizes and that he had approached these wives, passing himself off as being from Social Welfare. During his interviews with these women, he obtained money from them in return for the provision of various social services, which of course were never received. Passmore was arrested and charged with these offences of deception and appeared before Bristol Magistrates' Court once again, where he was sentenced to six months' imprisonment. He later appeared at Cardiff Magistrates' Court, in order to answer to the further offences committed on the railway involving the bogus coach trips.

7

The Railway Policeman
Faces Danger

Police officers, at the start of their duty, do not know what they may encounter during their shift. Most of the time it will be routine and uneventful, but they should be ready to deal with anything, drawing on their variety of experiences. They are also aware that they are on the front line and, at times, will find themselves in a position of danger, either knowingly or as the result of a rapidly developing situation. What begins as a routine enquiry, observation exercise or perhaps something out of the ordinary could result in them being injured, sometimes severely or even fatally. The following cases illustrate the extraordinary gallantry and bravery of railway police officers when faced with difficult and challenging situations.

When a Policeman's Instinct Lets him Down

A policeman uses his instinct and knowledge on many and varied occasions and is generally proved right in the assumptions they lead him to make. However, there are times when this lets him down, for whatever reason, and it can lead to a far worse situation than first expected. Such was the case for Police Constable William Leys, of the Midland Railway Company Police, in 1889.

On 12 July, PC Leys was on night duty, patrolling the Brent Sidings near to Child's Hill station, Hendon, in North London. At about 3 a.m. he saw a man, approximately 30 yards away from him, running towards an engine that was engaged in shunting wagons. Now this was not behaviour normally seen in a goods siding at such an early hour in the morning. PC Leys ran across the tracks and positioned himself between the man and the moving engine, shouting at him to stop. The man did so, but then turned and ran away; Leys immediately gave pursuit and caught up with his suspect, asking him what he was doing. Making no reply, the man stepped towards the moving engine. Leys stopped him again and advised him that there was no way through the sidings, to which his suspect replied that he knew his way around. Not satisfied with the man's behaviour and responses, Leys took hold of him and, after a struggle, managed to get him to a nearby telegraph office. Following some further questions, the man was identified as Philip Percy Spriggs, aged twenty-seven years, living at 5 Featherstone Buildings, Holborn and a clerk at a firm of solicitors in Bedford Row, London.

PC Leys formed the opinion that Spriggs may have been intent on committing suicide when he had apprehended him as he was trying to reach the moving engine. Having quietened the man down, he decided that he would need assistance and instructed the telegraph clerk, James Welch, to keep an eye on him. Spriggs was left sitting on a chair and, after a couple of minutes, he took a revolver out of his waistcoat pocket and pointed it at a very startled James Welch before firing a shot that, fortunately, was wide of the mark.

PC Leys was only a few yards away when he heard this shot and, on turning towards the sound, saw Welch running from the telegraph office; he then heard another. Leys ran towards the telegraph office and saw the door slam shut in front of him. Looking through a window, he could see Spriggs sitting in front of the door with a revolver held in both hands, pointing it directly at the door. Leys, with great courage and determination, went back to the door and burst it open, jumping on Spriggs while simultaneously seizing the revolver by the muzzle. The gunman, still grasping the revolver butt and trigger, shouted at Leys to let go or he would shoot him. A fierce struggle ensued, with the weapon being pointed at Leys on several occasions. At one point, Spriggs was able to turn the revolver fully on PC Leys and pull the trigger; the bullet went between the policeman's legs and lodged in the floor, so the struggle continued. In the meantime, Welch had raised the alarm and PC Thurlow arrived to assist at the scene. On hearing a shot and Leys shouts for help, he entered the office and immediately wrestled the revolver from Sprigg's hand. After a short tussle, Spriggs was restrained and quietened down.

The gun was still loaded and PC Leys went to the window of the office and fired the remaining bullets into the ground outside. As he was doing this, Spriggs got up suddenly and ran towards Leys, brandishing a sheath knife, but was disarmed by PC Thurlow before any harm could be done. Albeit belatedly, their assailant was then searched by the officers, who found a further five rounds of ammunition in his coat pocket and a cut-throat razor. Having confiscated these items and secured Spriggs safely, they called for the duty sergeant.

Sergeant Thomas Donaldson, also of the MRP, went to the telegraph office and took charge of the situation, questioning Spriggs. Donaldson asked him if he knew what he had been doing, and Spriggs said that he had. He also identified the revolver as his and said he had bought it in a shop in High Holborn earlier that day. Donaldson asked him, 'What did you intend doing with it?' Spriggs replied, 'I intended to shoot somebody, and to shoot myself afterwards; but I did not intend to shoot you', probably referring to PC Leys. He identified the knife as his and also the initials he had carved on the handle, admitting he would have used it should the revolver fail to fire. As for the razor, he said, 'There's nothing in that; that is no good at all.' PS Donaldson cautioned Spriggs and told him that he was being arrested and would be charged, to which he replied, 'You may as well give me some poison and have done with it at once.' He was then taken to the local police station and charged.

Philip Percy Spriggs appeared at the Old Bailey on 29 July and pleaded not guilty to the charge of feloniously shooting at William Leys, with intent to maim and to disable, and to do grievous bodily harm. Following the evidence of PCs Leys and Thurlow and PS Donaldson, the medical officer of Holloway Prison, Dr Philip Gilbert, gave evidence on the mental condition of Spriggs. He concluded, from the frequent examinations he had carried out, that he was insane and had been for some time. The defendant was intensely dejected and subject to the delusion that people were following him and were going to put him away. There was no history of alcoholism or drug misuse.

Spriggs was found guilty of the offence, but the court recognised that he was insane at the time and ordered that he be detained in a mental institution until Her Majesty's pleasure be known. As for PC William Leys, he owed his life twice to the swift action of his colleague PC Thurlow and no doubt would be more careful in the future, when acting on his instinct.

A Steady Nerve and a Cup of Tea

The Second World War in Europe was coming to an end, but the blackout was still in force and was a godsend for criminals, although the night of 4 April 1945 was looking to be a quiet one. Detective Sergeant William Parker Huddart, of the London, Midland & Scottish Railway Police, was on duty at the London Road passenger station, Leicester. At about 1.30 a.m. he informed the temporary police constable on duty that, as it was so quiet, he was going to the Queen Street goods depot to have a look around. When he arrived there, he was asked to telephone the police office at London Road station. He spoke to the TPC, who informed him that he had found a man trying car doors in the car park and had subsequently arrested him and taken him to the police office, and asked Huddart to return.

Huddart made his way back and walked up the platforms into the booking hall, where he was surprised to see uniformed officers of Leicester City Police. The TPC came up to him in a very excited state and, after Huddart had calmed him down, he told him that the man had been brought from the car park to the office and had then asked to go to the toilet, which was across the passage. He had allowed him to go and then spoken to Huddart on the telephone. The man returned to the office and immediately pulled a gun out of his overcoat pocket and shouted to the TPC to leave the office. Needless to say, he very quickly did and, while leaving, turned the office lights off. He then decided to get some backup and telephoned the City Police, who sent six uniformed constables to the station.

Huddart, being the senior officer on the scene, consulted with two of the City Police constables, PCs Kemshall and Arnold, and decided that he should go into the office to ascertain if what had been reported by the TPC was correct. PC Walter Arnold volunteered to accompany him. Huddart approached the office door and opened it with his key, then reached in and turned the lights on. Looking in, he saw a hand, holding a revolver, appear from a clothes rack and point towards the door. A voice shouted, 'Get out, I don't like policemen!' Huddart let the door come to and conferred with Arnold. The situation was dangerous but required immediate action, so he proposed to go into the office; Arnold urged him not do so, but Huddart disregarded this advice as, being in plain clothes, he felt he stood a good chance of talking the gunman into coming out. He told him to keep everyone else away, his reasoning being that, if they all went in, the gunman might panic and kill one or more officers. He then went into the room alone.

On entering, he immediately walked to the office desk opposite the clothes rack, where the gunman was still hiding. The gunman said, 'Don't move or I'll shoot.' Huddart looked round and saw the hand, still holding the gun, now pointing at him. He decided to play it calm and engage the gunman in conversation so asked his name, to which the reply was, 'You don't know me, but I know you. You are a detective sergeant.' Huddart quickly surveyed the office and saw two heavy calibre cartridges on the floor but the gunman had seen them too and said, 'Don't touch them, kick them here to me.' Huddart replied, 'No fear, I don't want my toes blown off!' and sought to engage the gunman further, while realising that he would gradually run out of things to talk about.

Seeing a kettle on the stove, and knowing the situation could easily worsen, Huddart thought quickly and asked the gunman if he would like a cup of tea, as he could do with one himself. The gunman, thinking the tea was already made, told him to put it by a locker near the door. Huddart explained that he had to fill the kettle with water, which he had to get from the sink in the toilet. The gunman allowed him to leave, and while he was filling the kettle, Huddart put PC Arnold, who was outside the toilet door, in the picture about what he intended to do. Returning with the kettle, he placed it on the gas ring and suddenly remembered he had come from home without tea or sugar. Knowing he had to play for time now, he turned the gas down very low.

Fifty minutes had now passed and Huddart realised that the only course of action would be for him to tackle the gunman, who was 12 feet away and had the gun pointed at him the whole time. The gunman asked whether Huddart would let him go if he laid the gun down; Huddart declined this request. The situation was now becoming intense and Huddart was running out of ideas. Then he noticed the gunman's identity card laying on the floor, which he had probably dropped when brought into the office for questioning. Huddart hit upon an idea. He carefully picked the ID card up and offered it to the gunman, telling him that he would need it if he was stopped by police; he held it out and walked towards the clothes rack. The gunman become nervous and said, 'Don't come any nearer, I've got seven rounds in and I'm keeping one for myself.' Huddart coolly replied, 'If you make a mess in there, my inspector will be very annoyed.' Still holding the card out, he managed to get very close to the gunman. The gunman motioned Huddart to put the card on a nearby chair. He realised that this would be his only chance of disarming the gunman and knew he had to act very quickly. He dropped the card on the chair, noting that the gunman was holding the gun in his left hand. He suddenly moved to his right to get to the gun, but the gunman immediately brought the gun up. Huddart had to change from a downward action, intended to knock the gun out of the gunman's hand, to one in an upwards direction, and as he hit the man's wrist, the gunman fired.

Huddart was so close to the gunman that he felt the blast in his left eye, and the bullet then went through his overcoat and jacket, just behind his left shoulder but, by a stroke of luck, did not injure him. He jumped the gunman and disarmed him, by which time the office became full of policemen and Huddart was able to arrest him. After the incident, it was discovered that the bullet that passed through Huddart's clothing had ricocheted, making a hole in a heavy uniform overcoat that was hanging up, gone through a wood partition, cut a broom handle in half, gouged a hole in the plaster of a wall and, finally, come to rest on the office carpet. The weapon used was a large German calibre Luger Automatic and six live rounds of high-penetration ability ammunition were found in the left-hand pocket of the gunman's overcoat.

The man, whose surname was Barnett, was charged with attempted murder and four other firearms-related offences and appeared at Leicester City Assizes, where the charge of attempted murder was dropped to one of carrying a firearm with intent to endanger life. The defendant's counsel attempted to belittle Huddart's actions but fell afoul of Judge McNaughton, who admonished him by saying that nothing could alter the fact that Huddart was a very brave man. The gunman was found guilty of the charges and his counsel made a very convincing case for leniency. The following day, the gunman was sentenced to six months' imprisonment. The judge commended Huddart for his bravery by saying in court, 'I consider Sergeant Huddart acted with very great courage indeed and with every consideration for Barnett. It was a brave action and I wish the matter to be brought to the notice of the appropriate railway authorities.'

On 5 October 1945, the *London Gazette* announced that DS Huddart had been awarded the King's Police & Fire Service Medal for Gallantry, known in police circles as the Policeman's VC. He attended Buckingham Palace on 26 February 1946 to receive his award from King George VI. DS Huddart was the only railway policeman to be awarded this medal in the force's long history.

The King's Police and Fire Medal for Gallantry group of Detective Sergeant Huddart.

An Explosive Situation

Ernest Stephen Lanaway had served in the army in the First World War between 1915 and 1918. Like many ex-servicemen, he was looking for a job that offered prospects and chose to join the London, Brighton & South Coast Railway Police on 11 March 1919 as a police constable. He remained with the force during its amalgamation with other railway companies in 1923, when they became the Southern Railway Police, continuing with them during the Second World War, and then with the British Transport Commission Police in 1949, serving at Battersea Wharf, London Bridge, Blackfriars and, finally, Hither Green sidings. Lanaway was a man who was happy in his work, enjoying patrolling the beat and content to go about his police duties cheerfully.

On 7 November 1950, PC Lanaway was patrolling the sidings at Hither Green, London, as he had done on more occasions than he cared to remember. While walking round, he routinely checked a covered wagon, labelled as containing explosives, and satisfied himself that all was in order. About an hour later, he was again in the area and noticed that smoke and flames were coming out of the same wagon. He quickly ran to the fire and, with a pocket knife he had with him, began cutting the ropes that were securing the cover. He tried to pull it back and pieces fell to the ground. Struggling to remove the cover, he climbed on board the wagon only to find it was double-sheeted. He continued working to remove it and then discovered that the contents were live shells; at the same time, his uniform overcoat had caught fire. He quickly removed his coat and continued to pull away pieces of the burning covers, throwing them onto the grass verge next to the wagon.

By this time, the fire had got a good hold, but Lanaway continued to throw pieces of burning cover off until it had all being removed. However, his problems were not over then; he noticed that the rope holding the shells was on fire, as were the inside boards of the wagon. He realised that he could no longer cope with the fire on his own and shouted for help. A shunter had arrived at this point and he coupled his locomotive to the wagons and then drove them to a nearby fire hydrant, where the fire was finally extinguished. The area surrounding the sidings was residential and, had the shells exploded, there could have been widespread damage and even death.

PC Lanaway suffered badly blistered hands and his overcoat was severely burned. Being the modest and quiet man that he was, he did not tell his family what had happened; his wife assumed that he had been careless with a cigarette and was annoyed with him. It was not until he received a letter, informing him that, due to his prompt action and complete disregard for his own personal safety and devotion to duty, he was to be awarded the British Empire Medal for Gallantry, did he tell his family of the incident. The award and citation were published in the *London Gazette* on 9 March 1951. He was fifty-five years old at the time of the incident.

Ernest Lanaway continued to serve in the British Transport Police before retiring in 1961, at the age of sixty-five years. He then worked as a security officer until he began to suffer from ill health. This brave and modest man passed away on 14 May 1967, at the age of seventy-one.

The Carlton Loop Case

18 November 1954 saw the beginning of a series of raids from stationary railway vans that would continue well into the following year. A van was relieved of a quantity of wine between Rossington and Bawtry, in South Yorkshire, where the train had stopped for about ten minutes. On 5 January 1955, a consignment of shoes, valued at £100, was stolen from a van at Black Carr Loop, near Doncaster. At the same location, on 9 February, a quantity of textiles and carpets were found in a field and were linked to a raid on another van near Black Carr. The British Transport Commission Police were on the case and, linking the three raids, decided to keep observations around the Black Carr Loop area. On 16 February, early in the morning, officers disturbed a group of five men, but, after a long and difficult

chase, the men managed to escape. Working with the West Riding Constabulary, officers of the BTC Police continued to investigate the raids in the hope that they could establish who was behind the crimes.

Despite the large area to be covered, observations were taken up at places likely to be targeted by thieves. On 24 March, two vans containing tobacco were raided at Estrick Loop, with the thieves taking a total of seventeen cartons; five of these were recovered, but the value of the other twelve cartons amounted to £700. A few weeks later, on 14 April, BTCP officers and a dog handler were patrolling at Dearne Junction, near Doncaster. They surprised a group of men attempting to raid the vans, who then began to run, so a police dog was unleashed and went off in pursuit. As it caught up with the raiders, one of them turned round and knocked the dog out, enabling them to make good their escape. Enquiries continued, and a link with a known man who had a violent reputation, Leonard 'Butch' Mangham, was established, but the police were unable to get solid evidence. During April and May, a series of similar raids were made in the Doncaster, Grimsby and Lincoln areas.

After the last one in May, there were no further raids and it looked as if the trail had gone cold. Observations were continued but without any further result. Following a meeting between senior officers of the BTCP and local constabularies, an agreement was made for the forces to co-operate in their attempts to find and arrest the criminals involved. On 19 August, a train arrived at Retford from Newark and a van attached to the train was found to have been raided, with a carton of tobacco being stolen. The train had stopped twice en route, at Carlton Loop for ten minutes and Tuxford Loop for eighteen minutes. Enquiries on this latest raid, like before, came to nothing. On 26 August, consignments of cigarettes, wines and spirits valued at £300 were stolen. An investigation revealed that the train had stopped at Carlton Loop for eight minutes, Tuxford Loop for thirty-two minutes and Markham Loop for seventeen minutes. The police decided to concentrate their observations within these locations.

On 8 September, BTPC officers, in groups of twos and threes, were located at the Carlton, Markham and Tuxford loops to keep observations. The Carlton Loop observations were maintained by Police Constable Derek Cook, from Grimsby, and PCs Sidney Metcalfe and Donald Norton, both from Newark, all in plain clothes. At about 12.30 a.m. the following morning, the Newark to Doncaster goods train pulled into Carlton Loop. The officers saw torch lights, and then heard the sound of van doors being opened and cartons being thrown to the ground. The officers moved from their observation position in order to arrest the thieves. The train set off at 12.45 a.m., leaving five men standing between the loop and the main line. One of the group began walking towards the Carlton Loop signal box, and then disappeared, never to be seen again. The officers now moved in to arrest the remaining four men, but they had other ideas and ran off, with the officers in pursuit. One of the men, later identified as Hirst, was brought down in a nearby lane. Struggling vigorously, he shouted for help and the others returned before a violent fight began, with the officers being obliged to draw their truncheons to protect themselves.

During the struggle, another of the gang, later identified as Arthur Mangham, attacked PC Norton using a steel hook attached to a rope, striking a violent blow to Norton's head, which resulted in the hook being embedded. Another man, later named as Bowen, took hold of Norton's truncheon and struck him on the back of the head. DC Metcalfe was also severely beaten with a heavy, lead-filled cane and was knocked unconscious; PC Cook was similarly beaten around the head but not to the point of unconsciousness. Despite his injuries, Norton managed to make his way to Sutton-on-Trent police station. The sergeant who lived there was out but his wife was at home and, on hearing Norton's cries for help, she found him covered in blood from head to foot; she rendered first aid and got a message to her husband for him to return. PC Cook managed to carry Metcalfe to a level crossing keeper's house and later went to help Norton. The officers were all eventually taken to Newark General Hospital for treatment.

Stunned by the news of the violent attacks, BTPC officers, along with colleagues from the Lincolnshire, Nottinghamshire and West Riding constabularies, began a search over a large area to find the gang. A watch was kept on Arthur Mangham's house in Mexborough and at 4.45 a.m. he returned then left again, and was seen burying a large steel hook, a leather belt and a pair of bolt croppers on a piece of waste land. When he left the scene, the items were dug up and Arthur Mangham was later arrested. He admitted that he had been train robbing but denied he had been at Carlton Loop, or in a fight with police officers. Leonard 'Butch' Mangham was stopped while riding a girl's bicycle that he had stolen; he said he had been poaching and knew nothing of the crime.

Packages from the railway van that had been handled by members of the gang were examined for finger prints; only a smudged and incomplete print was found, but it was good enough to provide a match with a man known as Jack Hirst, who was subsequently arrested. Eric Bowen, an associate of the men who had been arrested, was picked up when he returned from Blackpool and, when examined, was found to have bruising consistent with that caused by truncheon blows. Over the next few days, further evidence was found and used to build up a picture that tied the gang to the crime.

All four men were charged and appeared before Newark Magistrates' Court, where they pleaded not guilty and were committed for trial. On 22 November, appeared before Mr Justice Streatfield at the Nottingham Assizes. Once again, they all pleaded not guilty and the trial proceeded for four days. The judge summed up the case and sent the jury out to deliberate. After an hour and half, they returned, stating they could not come to a decision on Bowen's case. The judge gave them some guidance and sent them back. Two hours later, the jury returned with the news that they still could not decide about Bowen. He was ordered to stand trial again at the next assizes.

On 25 November, the Manghams and Hirst appeared for sentencing. Mr Justice Streatfield told Leonard Mangham that he was a complete menace to society and that it was his intention to keep him out of the public arena for some time; he also noted that he was too often involved in incidents of violence and railway theft only. The judge then sentenced him to fourteen years' imprisonment. Arthur Mangham was sentenced to eight years' imprisonment after being told by the judge that he too was a violent man, and it was only by luck he was not facing a charge of murder. Jack Hirst also received a similar sentence and was reprimanded by the judge. The judge then commended DC Metcalfe and PCs Cook and Norton saying, 'You behaved that night with the utmost devotion to duty and gallantry. I am sure that everyone who listened to this case will feel the utmost gratitude for the splendid service you rendered, not only to the railways but to the public.'

Their bravery was indeed recognised; the *London Gazette*, dated 26 January 1956, announced that DC Metcalfe and PCs Cook and Norton had been awarded the Queen's Commendation for Brave Conduct. The citation read,

'For services when a gang of violent and dangerous criminals attempted to rob a railway goods van.'

The rope and hook used by Arthur Mangham to assault Police Constable Donald Norton.

From left to right: Detective Constable (formerly Police Constable) Donald Norton, PC Derek Cook and DC Sidney Metcalf.

Eric Bowen stood trial again at the Nottingham Assizes on 27 February 1957, once more pleading not guilty. The trial lasted two days and, this time, the jury found him guilty. Mr Justice Ashworth sentenced Bowen to eight years' imprisonment.

A Stab in the Back

It was in the early hours of the morning, on 17 February 1956, that Police Constable Alexander Waterland was patrolling the goods yard at West Hartlepool station. Walking alongside the boundary wall that ran between the goods yard and the adjoining street, he heard a noise and, being curious, looked over the wall and saw two men near the goods office carrying suitcases. One man was tall, wearing a brown leather jerkin, and the other was much smaller, wearing a black leather jerkin plus a Russian-style, black leather hat with fur-lined ear muffs. Not happy about the situation, PC Waterland decided to investigate further and made his way towards the men, whereupon he stopped them and asked what they were doing.

The taller of the two men said that they had been with some women and their working clothes were inside the suitcases. He added that they were crewmen on a Swedish ship, berthed in Hartlepool Docks. This man's English was not good and PC Waterland had some trouble in understanding what he was being told. He asked the other man the same questions but did not receive any reply; however the men began to converse in their own language. While he was talking to the men, PC Waterland had noticed that the suitcases were new and appeared to be heavy.

Far from satisfied, he asked the men to accompany him to the police office, which they did without any trouble.

When they reached the police office, however, PC Waterland moved to one side to open the door and, as he did so, felt a heavy blow on his back, causing him to fall to his knees. Looking round, he saw the smaller of the men step back and run off, following his friend. He shouted for help and the duty sergeant and a PC, who were in the office at the time, came out and saw that PC Waterland had been stabbed in the left shoulder. The PC gave chase and managed to get close enough to the two men to recognise them; he had stopped them earlier in the night and had questioned them as they were leaving the docks and walking towards the town. He returned to the police office and called for an ambulance before helping the sergeant give first aid treatment to their injured colleague.

At the hospital, PC Waterland was examined and found to have a deep knife wound in his left shoulder, measuring one-and-a-quarter inches long, half an inch wide and one and three-quarters of an inch deep. As well as the wound, his scapula had been fractured by the knife blow. It was opined that the knife was double-bladed and the blow delivered with such extreme force that, if the knife had not been deflected by the scapula, the wound would have been fatal. The suitcases that had been left behind by the fleeing seamen were opened and found to contain various items of new clothing and shoes. The local police were informed of the incident and they confirmed that the clothing had been stolen from a gentleman's outfitters in the town.

Police Constable B84 Alexander Waterland.

Both the local force and British Transport Commission Police, armed with a good description of the two men, began intensive enquiries in Hartlepool Docks from the ships berthed there. Taking no chances, a police dog was brought along to help find the offenders. From these enquiries, the focus of the search moved to a German ship SS *Carl* and, with the permission of the captain, officers were taken to the crew's quarters, where the two men were found and identified by the officer who had given chase earlier that night. Through the services of an interpreter, the men were asked further questions and a search of the men produced a cigarette lighter, stolen from the shop, and suitcase keys. They were arrested and taken to the local police station, where they were identified as Hans Walter Schmidt, aged twenty-five years, and Gunter Dorsch, aged twenty years. Both were charged with wounding PC Waterland with intent to kill, and breaking and entering a shop and stealing goods to the value of £178 2s 4d; they were then committed to stand trial.

Schmidt and Dorsch appeared at Leeds Assizes before Mr Justice Donovan and pleaded not guilty to attempted murder. Dorsch pleaded guilty to a lesser charge of wounding with intent to resist arrest and was sentenced to seven years' imprisonment. Both men pleaded guilty to breaking and entering and stealing goods, for which they were sentenced to two years' imprisonment. It was established that they both had criminal records in Germany; Judge Donovan told the men that the use of a knife on a policeman would not be tolerated in this country and, even though he accepted that they did not have any intention of using the weapon at the outset of the evening, he could only take a serious view of the charges.

PC Waterland made a full recovery and continued in his police career, retiring in June 1984 having completed thirty-four years' service.

Bravery Above and Beyond the Call of Duty

When a police officer goes on duty, he or she does not know what they may encounter. Although they always strive to prepare for the unknown, when an incident occurs, it can still take them by surprise. In this case, an act of anti-social behaviour turned out to have catastrophic consequences for a police officer.

Ronald McKoy was 6 feet, 4 inches tall, weighed 16 stone, suffered from a mental health illness and was a violent man. He had a pathological hatred of the police and had attacked a police officer and killed a police dog with a machete. He was considered so dangerous that he was kept in a secure mental unit, where he received treatment for his illness. On 1 December 2001, McKoy absconded from the unit and, having had no medication, he was in a highly dangerous, volatile condition and was wandering the streets of London. His last known address in London was being visited by Metropolitan Police officers in full riot uniform in order to protect themselves, hoping to find him. However, while this was taking place, McKoy was elsewhere and the incident took an unexpected turn.

At 1 p.m. British Transport Police Inspector Michael Tanner, known to his colleagues as Dan, was returning to the police station at Finsbury Park Underground station, London. As he got out of his marked police vehicle, he saw a man walk over to the vehicle and begin urinating on it. Inspector Tanner, not surprisingly, remonstrated with McKoy, who responded by saying, 'I'm going to kill you.' Smiling, he put his hands inside his coat and produced a large commando knife and then moved quickly towards Inspector Tanner, who immediately drew his extendable baton to defend himself. McKoy lunged into the inspector, which caused his police utility belt to unbuckle and fall off, putting his handcuffs and radio beyond reach.

By now, there were a crowd of onlookers, who saw McKoy attempting to stab the inspector, who in turn was trying to defend himself with his baton. Many of the onlookers were shocked by what was happening and ran away from the scene. A furious fight took place and the inspector managed to strike McKoy several times and, although exhausted, he was gaining the advantage when McKoy stabbed him in the chest, causing a two-and-a-half-inch deep wound. Inspector Tanner saw his shirt become soaked in blood and realised that he had been badly wounded; knowing that he would not be able to continue defending himself, he turned away from his assailant and began to run. McKoy chased after the officer and, when he had caught up with him, plunged the knife into his right arm. With difficulty, Inspector Tanner managed to free himself and, with great effort, sprinted towards a nearby, empty bus whose doors were open and climbed on board. The driver, who had been shocked by what he had witnessed, took what seemed an age before closing the doors, just as McKoy was attempting to follow the inspector on to the bus. He made frenzied attempts to force the doors open and used his knife to try and cut through the rubber edging. Inspector Tanner told the driver, who was by now in a traumatised state, to pull away, but he stalled the bus engine several times before, eventually, managing to drive off. McKoy chased the bus for a short distance before giving up. Unfortunately, he then turned his attention towards passers-by and grabbed a fourteen-year-old girl, holding the knife to her throat.

Inspector Tanner, who was looking through the bus window, saw what McKoy had done. No police support had yet arrived, so he opened the bus doors and leapt out, shouting at McKoy. He was hoping to distract him and it had the desired effect; McKoy let the girl go and chased after him instead. The inspector now had to play for time. He knew that assistance would have been summoned and was probably on its way, but he did not know how long it would take for help to arrive. Although severely wounded and bleeding, he played a game of cat and mouse; when McKoy stopped running after him, he would turn back and walk towards him, enticing McKoy to continue with his pursuit. Inspector Tanner, now extremely weak from loss of blood and gasping for breath, managed to keep a safe distance until officers from the Metropolitan Police arrived with riot shields. They were able to subdue McKoy, but not before he had stabbed two officers, one in the leg and the other in the stomach.

All three wounded officers were given medical treatment at the scene and taken to hospital, where Inspector Tanner remained for three days. He was off work for nine months, recovering from his wounds and the ordeal that he had endured.

In March 2003, McKoy appeared at the Central Criminal Court before Mr Justice Gerald Gordon, charged with attempted murder and affray; he pleaded guilty to all the charges and was sentenced to life imprisonment. At the conclusion of the trial, the judge made the following statement of commendation: 'Inspector Tanner acted with a bravery going well beyond the call of duty. Having been stabbed twice with a vicious-looking knife, he deliberately put himself back in danger. I rarely commend officers and do so only in exceptional circumstances – these are exceptional circumstances.'

On 29 November 2004, the following announcement appeared in the *London Gazette*:

> The Queen has been graciously pleased to approve the following award of The Queen's Gallantry Medal to Michael Tanner, Inspector, British Transport Police.

He was invested with the medal by Her Majesty the Queen at Buckingham Palace in March 2005. Inspector Michael 'Dan' Tanner QGM is still a serving officer with the British Transport Police.

Finsbury Park Underground station and bus stand, where Inspector Michael Tanner was attacked.

Inspector Michael 'Dan' Tanner (right) receiving a commendation from Chief Superintendent Paul Brogan in November 2015.

8

The Lighter Side of the Railway Policeman's Work

The policeman encounters every facet of life during the course of his career; it has been said that this is what makes a policeman's work so interesting. On different occasions, the officer will encounter moments of sadness, fear, amusement and the hum-drum of everyday life. One of the most important assets that an officer can have is a sense of humour – natural or developed, it matters not. Even in difficult and demanding circumstances, this ability to see the funny side can defuse a situation or give a sense of relief after a stressful time. The following cases, both routine and out of the ordinary, are but a few examples where the outcome had an amusing slant that brought a dimension of humour to what is, at times, a difficult and demanding occupation.

Shadows in the Dark

It is not unusual for police officers to work together, especially in the CID. Such was the case with two experienced detectives who had known and worked with each other for more years than either of them cared to remember. Police humour being what it is, they were known as Mutt and Jeff and both revelled in the status that had been accorded to them, playing along with the stories that abounded.

There had been a series of thefts from wagons in the station goods yard and it soon came around to the turn of Mutt and Jeff to keep observations in the yard. It was a very dark and chilly night when they commenced this duty and, after some hours, having only seen shadows and heard the rustle of tarpaulins in the breeze, they had become bored, cold and cramped. They decided that they should move to another position in the yard and stretch their legs at the same time.

As they stealthily made their way across the yard, Mutt spotted someone walking slowly, crossing a field towards the railway boundary fence. The two detectives crouched down and saw the suspect make their way across the field, stop, move forward and then stop again. They watched the suspect for fifteen minutes, not moving a muscle in case they were spotted. The suspect was now close to the fence and had not moved for a while, and the detectives became bored with waiting, Mutt suggested that they should separate and make their way to the fence, then jump over and apprehend the suspect, taking a chance on the outcome.

The two intrepid officers moved cautiously towards the fence, waited, then jumped over and ran towards the suspect. The suspect turned around in fear and galloped off into the darkness, never to be seen again. Yes, the suspect was a young horse belonging to a farmer whose field ran alongside the goods yard. Mutt and Jeff looked at each other and laughed until they were hoarse!

The Hole Truth

Police officers encounter many strange things in the course of their careers, and perhaps this incident is one of the strangest.

One cold, damp and misty night, a telephone call was received by the duty officer at the Bricklayers Arms goods depot, South London. It was from a railway worker in Greenwich, who said, 'Someone's dug a hole.' The officer repeated what he thought he had heard and received the reply, 'Yes guv, a hole, right next to the sub-station,' before the caller rang off. As it was a somewhat strange telephone call, the officer relayed the message to his colleague. Taking into account the inclement weather, and not really wanting to venture out, they wondered if this was a prank call from one of their off-duty colleagues, policeman's humour being what it is. Deciding that they had better check out the information received, they wrapped up and ventured forth.

On their arrival at the sub-station at Greenwich, they found a hole – not just an ordinary hole, but a professionally dug, sheer, 4-by-4 foot hole. Looking into it, they discussed the possibilities of the hole being prepared to dump a body in, as a tunnel to gain entry into the sub-station, or even as a place to put stolen property. Not knowing quite how to proceed, they went to the local police station to see if they knew anything about the hole and how that might fit in with information they already had. The response they received was very much like their own on taking the original phone call. After some discussion, the station sergeant, who had been eating one of his five-a-day, decided that the matter was best left to the CID.

The following night, the officers returned to Greenwich police station to be greeted by a less-than-happy detective sergeant who, after a few strong expletives, explained that he had contacted his detective inspector at home, who had then got out of bed to visit the scene. The disgruntled DS, having had his ears strongly bent by his superior, went on to add that he thought his chances of promotion had now been well and truly buried, possibly in the mystery hole. As he walked away he added, 'By the way, it's got bigger, your hole, it's got bigger!'

The hole became the centre of conversation and subsequent visits showed the hole getting larger each time. Further enquiries were made and observations undertaken, but without any results. The mystery hole had, by now, become famous in its own right and the Bricklayers Arms' officers were ribbed unmercifully by their colleagues. The hole continued to get bigger and deeper and then, suddenly, on a routine visit, was found to have been filled in! Despite enquiries, neither the identity of the digger, nor the reason the hole had been dug and then filled in, was ever found. So the case of the mystery hole was never solved; but there can be no doubt that all those involved in investigating the matter had told the whole truth when submitting their reports to senior officers.

The Smell of Success?

One morning, in June 1941, a group of six Irishmen boarded the train at Heysham, intending to travel to London. The train stopped at Lancaster for a while and the Irishmen, taking advantage of the stop, went into the refreshment room and placed their order with the female counter assistant. While she had her back to them, the men turned around a glass case on the counter that contained various brands of cigarettes, grabbing about 200 packets, then ran out onto the platform and jumped onto their train as it was moving off. The assistant turned around as they were leaving and called out to them, just as they were boarding the train. She telephoned the nearest British Transport Commission Police office, which was in Preston, and informed them of what had happened. The train was due to pull into Preston station at 11.30 a.m.

The call was taken by the duty detective inspector who gathered a detective sergeant, a detective constable and a probationary police constable. When the train arrived, they all boarded and began searching the train for the culprits, with the PC leading the way. He came to a compartment, where the Irishmen were sitting surrounded by a large amount of cigarette ash, stubs and packets. Sliding the compartment door open, the constable saw a large quantity of unopened cigarette packets under the seats. The constable informed them that he was arresting them for the theft of cigarettes and ordered them to leave the compartment. Naturally, the Irishmen refused and they began to make the officer's task difficult; the tables were turned, however, when the two CID officers appeared behind him.

The six men were taken to the police office on the station and a call was made to the local police, requesting transport to take the men to Preston police station to be charged. Two uniformed duly officers arrived with a van, both wearing revolvers as this was war time. The men were led away to the van and an awful stench was noticed emanating from the group. Later it was learned that, when the men saw the revolvers, they genuinely thought they were going to be shot for looting and, consequently, five of them had filled their pants!

A case where the criminals definitely did not come up smelling of roses and the policemen had the last laugh, albeit a stifled one, due to them having to hold their noses!

The Plastered Policeman

Policemen have had bad fortune wished on them from time to time; it goes with the territory and no notice is ever taken of it. However, there are occasions that can lead them to wondering if there may be something to worry about after all.

One such case involved a man, who shall be known as Joe Bloggs, who left his village to find employment in the nearest city, where work was plentiful. He found a job and, for several weeks, enjoyed the satisfaction of earning a large pay packet at the end of each week. Eventually, the contract his employers were engaged on finished and Joe Bloggs found himself unemployed once again. He decided that he would return home and the only way available to him was to use the railway; fares were expensive and, in his view, unnecessary. If he could save some money, he would.

Joe thought about how he could reduce the money a train ticket would cost and, after studying the timetable, worked out a plan to avoid paying the full fare. This meant him changing at a particular station, which was pivotal to the success of the plan. His journey went well until he went to change at the station which, since his last visit home, had been closed down. He was challenged by a ticket inspector, who took his name and address and was cursed by Joe for his interest. The local British Transport Commission Police office was informed and an officer was sent to interview Joe at his home. This officer was similarly abused and cursed by Joe once he found that he would be summoned for ticket irregularities.

The day of the hearing arrived, and all parties turned up at the magistrates' court, which was in a distant part of the county and meant the police officer had needed to stay overnight in a bed and breakfast; he in turn wished Joe a fate worse than death, as this overnight stay had caused an argument with his wife, something he didn't need. The officer was called to the witness stand and took the Bible in his right hand, swearing the oath, and as he put the good book down, a large piece of plaster fell from the ceiling and hit him on the head!

Had Joe's wish for a curse on the officer come true, or was it just a coincidence. We will never know.

A Welsh Rarebit

In October 1966, a uniformed constable of the British Transport Police was patrolling his beat, which included the forecourt of Cardiff General railway station. It was on this forecourt that he espied a car parked in a No Parking Zone and duly took down the details of the vehicle in his pocket book. Consequently, a summons was applied for and served on the owner of the car, who happened to be a twenty-one-year-old teacher at a local primary school.

A few days later, after the summons had been served, the officer received a letter but was unable to read it, as it appeared to him to be in a foreign language. He showed it around the police office in the hope that someone may be able to translate it for him. No one could, but it was the general consensus of opinion that the language was Welsh. The dilemma soon came to the attention of the divisional superintendent, who could speak and read Welsh, and he translated the letter, the contents of which requested that all communications to the defendant should be in the Welsh language. This raised the question as to whether this was in order and, following a consultation with the clerk to the magistrates' court, it was found to be correct.

The police now had to re-apply for the summons and this, and all the documentation that accompanied it, had to be written in Welsh; the divisional superintendent was kept busy for a few days, to say the least. Eventually the summons and documentation in Welsh was served on the school teacher. Nothing more was thought of the matter and there it rested until the day of the hearing.

At the hearing at Cardiff Magistrates' Court, the guilty plea form was entered and accepted but the defendant had written her mitigating circumstances in Welsh. The officer and court officials were at a loss now, as there was no one in the court who could read or speak the language. An adjournment was given in order for the divisional superintendent to attend court and act as an interpreter. Having taken the interpreter's oath, he read out the mitigating circumstances to the court and the defendant was fined £10.

The case was over and maybe the reporting officer wished he had never booked the defendant; the superintendent probably thought he should have been paid the court interpreter's fee, which he did not receive. Both may have privately thought that the defendant knew exactly what she was doing and was, in fact, the only one who saw the funny side of the chaos she caused!

He So Wanted to be a Policeman

During September 1967, an angry woman entered the police office at Derby and asked to see the senior officer as she had a serious complaint to make. The duty inspector at the time saw her and listened to what she had to say. It transpired that her son and his friend had been stopped for drinking, in Langley Mill, Derbyshire, by a man purporting to be a British Transport Police officer. She arrived at the scene shortly after and the man had produced a BTP warrant card, or what she had thought was one. The man threatened the boys with a good thrashing and from his demeanour she had assumed that he was, in fact, a police officer. Her main complaint was that she was far from happy with his disgraceful behaviour.

Complaints about police officers are taken seriously and an investigation was initiated immediately. From enquiries made, it appeared that the boys involved, aged fifteen and sixteen years, had been to the cinema and had arrived in Langley Mill at about 11 p.m. before starting to make their way home. It was then that the 'police officer' drove up to them in a sports car and accused them of drinking and jay-walking, telling them he was a BTP officer. The following day, the same officer arrived at the home of one of the boys and produced a warrant card. In the presence of the father, he told the boy he was going to give him a good thrashing and the man was so convincing that the boy agreed to this, rather than appear in court. Other similar incidents occurred over the following weeks and were fully investigated but there was never enough evidence to make any progress on the matter. The man became known in the locality as the 'railway policeman' and his description was exaggerated, so he became a monster, over 6 feet tall and built like a wrestler.

Several weeks later, three boys were on a disused railway line, looking for dandelions to feed their rabbits, when the 'policeman' turned up. He got them to empty their bags and then stand with their arms up against a wagon while he searched them. He produced his warrant card to impress upon the boys who he was and told them to come back the following day. However, one of the boys was an observant lad and made a note of the name and photograph on the card. The next day, the boys turned up, as arranged, but they had brought one of their fathers with them. The 'policeman' was very convincing, especially when he got into his sports car and spoke into a microphone, pretending to contact his station. The father was then completely taken in and was certain that the man was a police officer.

The incidents were reported to the BTP who, now having been given a name, made further enquiries and arrested 'the monster' – who turned out to be just over 5 feet tall, of very slim build and weak character! During the interview, the man admitted that it had all started out as a joke and even some of his friends from a local public house thought he was a BTP officer. One of his friends worked for the railway and had shown him his privilege ticket identity card, which the 'policeman' took off him, on some pretence or other. He altered the card by sticking green paper, which read 'BRITISH TRANSPORT POLICE', over the job grade description of the owner and then put a small photograph of himself on the card. He was charged with the impersonation of a police officer, the meaning of which he did not seem to understand; all he had wanted to be was a Special Constable and he had put the photograph on the card and pretended to be a BTP officer, just for a laugh.

The man appeared before Nottingham Magistrates' Court and pleaded guilty to two charges of impersonation of a police officer, one having taken place in Derbyshire and the other in Nottinghamshire. He was fined £30 and was admonished by the magistrates for his behaviour and the distress he had caused his victims. The defendant did not find his actions quite so amusing now and, indeed, it was the real policemen who had the last laugh.

No Room at the Inn

It was the season of goodwill – Christmas. A certain British Transport Police CID officer at Cardiff station had come to the end of his shift. It was 2 a.m. on a cold December morning and thoughts of going home to a warm bed and sleep were all that occupied him when he said goodnight to the constable at the front desk. As he was walking to the door, it opened and a well-dressed man came in and went up to the desk. In a sad voice, he announced, 'I want to give myself up.' The detective turned around and looked at the constable who looked back as if to say, 'Over to you.' With a groan, the detective walked back to the desk and asked, 'Give yourself up for what?' The man replied to this question with another, 'Can we go somewhere private?' He was guided into the CID office, where the detective assessed this possible criminal as a man who had been drinking and wanted to come clean, but he was neither drunk, nor did he smell of drink. This did not bode well and any thoughts of going home to bed quickly disappeared.

'Now what's this all about?' the detective asked, once they had been seated and as he was lighting a cigarette. The man shuffled in the chair and said, 'I've committed a terrible crime, officer.' The detective thought to himself, 'Here it comes; he's murdered someone.' However, he could not believe his ears when he heard the man say, 'I stole a carton of fishcakes this morning, in Cardiff.' He retorted, 'Fishcakes! Is that all?' The man replied, 'Yes, but stealing is a serious crime, isn't it?' The detective stifled a giggle and asked him the usual questions, where, when and why. The conclusion from the interview was that the man had stolen the fishcakes as he didn't have anywhere to live and he had the intention of giving himself up in order to get locked up.

As the crime had been committed off railway property, a phone call was made to the Cardiff City Police, who sent a car to pick him up. While waiting for the car to arrive, the friendly criminal became worried as he had thrown away the carton of fishcakes in the grounds of Cardiff Castle and, as it had not been found, there went the evidence to corroborate his confession. The detective suggested he wrote a statement and, when it was completed, he gave it to the local police officers. The next day, the man appeared in front of the Cardiff Stipendiary Magistrate, who, on hearing that he had no home, no family or friends and had previous convictions, did him a favour and sentenced him to six weeks' imprisonment; much to his delight, as he would now spend Christmas in prison and have a warm cell of his own and a Christmas dinner.

Several weeks later, the detective was on observation duties at Newport station when the fishcake thief saw him and immediately went up and shook his hand, saying, 'Thank you very much for locking me up. I had a wonderful Christmas with roast pork and all the trimmings for Christmas dinner. It was really great.' Taken aback, and a little annoyed that his cover may have been broken, the detective gave a reply that he felt fitted the situation, 'Try and stay out of trouble in future. It won't do you any good but if you do get in bother, come and see me.' The next night, the detective was at his desk, completing some paperwork, when the telephone rang. After the call, he replaced the receiver, sat back in his chair and laughed out loud saying, 'Ah well, you can't win them all!' The caller, an officer at Newport police station, was contacting him on behalf of a man who had been arrested that night, having given himself up to a police constable after admitting he had broken into a kiosk, by the Newport County football ground, and stolen goods.

Caught in a Web of Fear

For the duty signalman Dave, at the Bradford Road signal box at Shipley, 22 August 1989 started out as just an ordinary day. During his shift, he made himself a cup of tea and, afterwards, went to the sink to wash his cup up. It was then that he froze in horror. In the sink was, in his words, a two-and-a-half inch, smooth-backed, brown spider. He had seen spiders before, but nothing as large as this particular specimen. Frozen to the spot, he began to wonder if the spider had escaped from somebody's collection or from the zoo; he remembered stories of such spiders being found in bunches of bananas that had been imported into the country. With this in mind, he steeled himself and ushered the spider into an empty coffee jar and then sat down, shaking like a leaf.

Wondering what he should do now, he picked up the telephone and dialled the emergency number for the British Transport Police, begging them to come and take away this monster spider. A constable was despatched from Bradford to the scene to calm the terrified signalman and deal with the situation. When he arrived, the signalman pointed to the coffee jar containing the spider that had caused so much trouble. Expecting to see a huge spider of unknown origins, he had to smile to himself when he saw the spider was only half an inch in diameter!

Having calmed down the signalman, he left with the offending spider and took it to the local RSPCA office who gave the all clear. It was set free to wander away, without as much as a caution for terrifying the signalman. The story made the tabloid press under the headline 'Daffy Dave Goes Loco Over Spider'. The officer had made a statement to the reporters saying, 'I've seen bigger spiders in my bath. He made it sound like some sort of monster on the phone, but when we got there it was only about half an inch across.'

The officer, no doubt, took the incident as all part of a day's work and an example of the excitement of not knowing what he would face, every time he went on duty.

Cartoon by Park published in the *British Transport Police Journal* in the 1960s.

Also available from Amberley Publishing

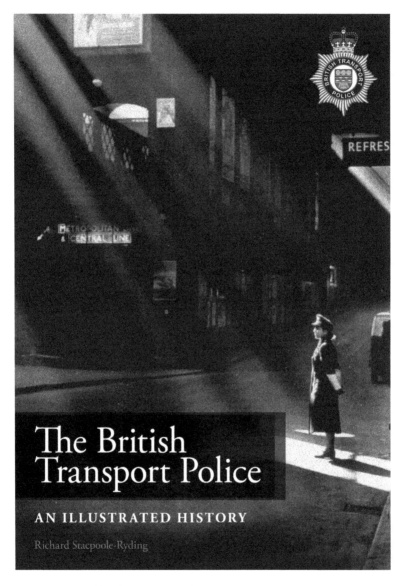

Available from all good bookshops or to order direct
Please call **01453–847–800**
www.amberley-books.com

TRACKING THE
HOOLIGANS
THE HISTORY OF FOOTBALL VIOLENCE
ON THE UK RAIL NETWORK

MICHAEL LAYTON
ALAN PACEY

Also available from Amberley Publishing

POLICE DOG HEROES

MICHAEL LAYTON & BILL ROGERSON